THIS TIME TOGETHER

STANLEY A. ROCK

ZONDERVAN
PUBLISHING HOUSE   OF THE ZONDERVAN CORPORATION
GRAND RAPIDS, MICHIGAN 49506

THIS TIME TOGETHER: A Guide to Premarital Counseling
Copyright © 1978 by Reformed Church Press
Revised edition copyright © 1980 by The Zondervan Corporation

Library of Congress Cataloging in Publication Data

Rock, Stanley A
   This time together.

   Bibliography: p.
   1. Marriage counseling. 2. Group relations training. I. Title.
HQ10.R58   1980   362.8'2   79-24874
ISBN 0-310-39171-7

Printed in the United States of America

Contents

Therefore, a man leaves his father and his mother and cleaves to his wife, and they become one flesh.

—*Genesis* 2:24

Foreword

Once upon a time, anyone who decided to own a car was free to take it out on the highway, fiddle with the controls, and learn to drive by trial and error. But automobile accidents are hazardous to life and limb; so it made sense to prevent them, as far as possible, by requiring a test before issuing a driver's license.

The wreckage of a broken marriage can be just as devastating to human well-being as that of a crashed car; and the marriage breakdown rate in our culture has now reached appalling proportions. We do what we can, by providing marriage counseling services, to help those in serious trouble—but often this proves to be too little or too late. The need to provide *preventive* services for couples, both before they marry and in their first critical year together, calls for action that is long overdue.

Some beginnings have been made. Programs for marriage preparation have been initiated by a number of pastors, and they are to be congratulated on their well-meaning efforts. Unfortunately, however, a number of recent researches—particularly those of Claude Guldner, Edward Bader, and David Olson—have made follow-up studies of some of the couples concerned and have discovered that the traditional preparation process they had gone through produced no significant results.

Closer examination has led to two important conclusions. First, the programs studied were largely *didactic*—they sought to provide *information* through talks, books, films, or discussions. Second, there was little or no follow-up after the wedding.

It now seems clear that giving out information about marriage, before the couple actually *experience* it, is of quite limited value in itself. What is needed is a *dynamic* approach—providing a setting in which the couple can immediately *apply*, together in their relationship, new knowledge that is being offered to them. If they can be helped to *try out* the new ways of interacting, get the feel of them, and make a commitment together to change their behavior in order to adapt creatively to each other, then something really happens.

For this to take place, however, we have to provide them with a special environmental setting. What couples need most of all, in order to grow, is the stimulus and support of other couples who will provide *models* for them, so that they can clearly perceive what they want their own relationship to become. The field of experiential education has taught us that effectiveness dramatically increases as we move up from *information* to *demonstration* to *participation*. This may sound like some exciting new educational discovery. In fact, it was embodied in an old Chinese proverb—"When I hear, I forget; when I see, I remember; when I act, I understand" —which is said to date from the fifth century B.C.!

We as a couple have for some years been deeply interested in promoting this new kind of learning for living, and applying it in the vital area of marriage preparation. In 1972 these ideas were embodied in the book, *Getting Ready For Marriage*, which tried to give the engaged couple tasks they could carry out together, as well as knowledge. However, since that time rapid progress has been made, and we are now aware that the couple alone may not be sufficiently motivated to carry this process far enough for it to be fully effective.

Our heavy involvement in marriage enrichment in recent years has brought the insights we lacked in 1972. We are now convinced that the ideal environment for experiential learning is created by gathering engaged couples into small sharing groups, skillfully led where possible by a mature married couple who are ready to share their own experience—their struggles as well as their achievements—and who know how to facilitate open sharing and experiential action in the group as a whole.

This is essentially what Stanley Rock is talking about in this book; and we heartily welcome it as a tangible token of the advent of a new era. The marriage preparation workshop, as described in these pages, is based on the concepts and practices that will, we believe, enable us at last to develop really effective preventive services for married couples.

We therefore warmly commend this book to all who have the responsibility and the privilege of guiding couples as they move into the great adventure of the shared life. We believe that, on the foundation laid in these pages, we can in the coming years build a far better approach to marriage preparation than we have ever had before. And we further believe that this should enable us to continue with these couples, after the wedding, and to see their relationship well and truly launched, so that in their later years together they will grow steadily toward the achievement of their full relational potential.

Then, and only then, the heavy toll of marriage breakdowns will at last begin to diminish, and we shall see a welcome increase of truly happy families, based upon richly fulfilled marriages.

DAVID AND VERA MACE
*Founders and Presidents
of the Association of
Couples for Marriage
Enrichment (ACME)*

Preface

A number of significant books and manuals on marriage preparation have been published in the last five years. The religious community has taken the leadership in this field, as pastors, campus ministers, and religious educators have recognized the great need for experientially based educational materials which concentrate on building effective couple relationships.

This Time Together is presented as a contribution for professionals and lay leaders who wish to explore the small-group approach to marriage preparation. There is no substitute for the kind of relationship built between a pastor and an individual couple in premarital counseling. Yet no marriage can be built in a vacuum. The small-group approach carefully developed and illustrated in this book provides the kind of supportive community in which couples may help each other to grow. We talk a great deal in the church about Christian fellowship, but where do we provide models for young couples who wish to build a companionship marriage? Again and again in such small-group workshops, participant couples have highlighted the importance of honest communication not only with each other but with other couples as well.

Every group leader will develop his or her own workshop model with its distinctive style. This book offers a way to get started, gives important help and training to group leaders, provides a complete workshop design and a participant's log with theological reflection and an extensive bibliography of resources.

The chapter entitled "A Personal Experience" is the work of Del and Trudy Vander Haar. Del is a staff executive in the Western Region for the Reformed Church in America, specializing in family life ministries. Trudy is a writer and Christian educator. They have written a beautiful statement of the meaning of marriage for their son and daughter-in-law.

This Time Together is dedicated to my colleague and friend, Dr. T. Nicholas Tormey, and Nancy Rupp Rock, my wife and companion, both of whom developed with the author various small-group models for marriage preparation and marriage enrichment through six years of campus ministry at Drake University, Des Moines, Iowa.

Acknowledgments

The author is sincerely grateful for permission granted by publishers for use of the following:

"The Marriage Expectation Inventory, Form I: For Engaged Couples," copyright © 1976. Reprinted by permission of Family Life Publications, Inc., Saluda, North Carolina. The Inventory is prepared by Patrick J. McDonald, Ellen B. Pirro, and Charles Cleveland.

Reaching Out: Interpersonal Effectiveness and Self-Actualization, copyright © 1972. Reprinted by permission of Prentice-Hall, Inc., Englewood Cliffs, New Jersey.

"The Premarital Communication Inventory" and "Tuning In to Yourself" by Millard J. Bienvenu, Sr., Department of Sociology and Social Work, Northwestern State University of Louisiana.

"Agreement Statements for Groups" by Patrick J. McDonald, Human Service Associates, Des Moines, Iowa.

The author is also grateful to Henry Kleinheksel, Emeritus Assistant to the President at Western Theological Seminary, for assistance with financial forms in chapter 7, "Additional Resources."

CHAPTER
1

The
Small-Group
Approach

CHAPTER **1**

The Small-Group Approach

"A couple of sessions with the minister" is probably the classic model of marriage preparation. One couple works together with a single counselor—usually the pastor who will perform the ceremony—over a period of time, discussing aspects of their present and future relationship.

Under ideal circumstances there are certainly some benefits to such individualized attention. Circumstances, however, are not often ideal, especially in the busy weeks before a wedding. What might have been extremely helpful sessions, tailored to the specific needs of the couple, often turn out to be rushed and awkward for counselor and couple alike.

The author has found, in a half-dozen years of experimenting with various models of marriage preparation, that a small-group approach offers its own unique advantages to persons planning marriage. This manual is prepared for use in small-group situations. The following, introductory remarks sketch out some suggestions for leaders who may have only a little experience working with such groups.

1. Why Small Groups?

The value of the small-group marriage preparation workshop lies in the dawning recognition on the part of those involved that marriage—the most intimate of human relationships—does not happen in a vacuum. Romantic ballads to the contrary, two people don't build a world of their own, shutting out all else, when they get married. For Christian couples planning to marry, this realization is intensified by the knowledge that their relationship will develop within a Christian community, which is committed to helping them grow. A small-group workshop can be an intensive foretaste of that process.

High-flown sentiments? Perhaps. But there are some important practical examples of how this process works. A couple in a small-group marriage preparation workshop will soon learn that other couples share many of the same questions, problems, and worries about the commitment they are about to make to each other. This couple will be reassured to discover that the need for problem solving does not doom a relationship to failure, and they will learn—both positively and negatively—how other couples face their difficulties. As the session goes on, an atmosphere of openness and trust will develop, and increased honesty will result. The group as a whole will become a sounding board for all the participating couples. In many cases the members can point out how a person might be failing to listen to or might be misunderstanding a partner. Individuals will often dare to bring up issues they would never risk raising alone with their partners. All of this interaction can support the individual counseling which the pastor will undertake with each couple.

Not all the benefits of a workshop will be immediately obvious. Good communication takes time—and practice—to grow, particularly when well-entrenched habits of bad communication must first be recognized and then unlearned. The encouragement of others will help support one's beginning steps in listening, expressing ideas and feelings, and responding sympathetically. Being in a situation where one must talk about some of the most important ideas and values he or she holds will require many people to think harder and examine themselves more searchingly than ever before. In some cases there will be sharp and significant differences of opinions and values among the people taking part; and for many people, confronting these differences firsthand may strengthen their own ideas and at the same time broaden their appreciation for those of others. There can be no doubt that this sort of dealing constructively with differences is at the heart of happy and growing marriages.

Effective small-group marriage preparation programs do not just happen because a group of couples with good intentions decide to spend a weekend together. As suggested above, the small group is not meant to be the only source of premarital learning the couple has. The amount of individual counseling a couple needs will vary, but all couples should plan for some sessions with a pastor in addition to the group experience. Within the workshop itself, as well, there must be some time for couples to spend together alone in order for them to personalize some of the things they have heard and experienced while they are learning them.

It's important that a small group be *small*. We have found that six or seven couples planning marriage, along with one man and one woman as facilitators, is an ideal size. If there are more than seven couples, it is possible to have concurrent groups, provided there are enough leaders available. The size of each group, however, should allow all participants to contribute frequently and to develop trusting relationships with all the others.

Finally, the group program cannot be expected to succeed if the leadership is not effective. For many of the participants this will be a completely new experience, full of pitfalls both imagined and real; the leader must be sensitive to their apprehensions. Obviously, each new workshop will find the attentive leader better prepared for the unexpected than the last; but if experience is the best teacher, it is certainly not the only one, nor need it be only our personal experience which teaches us. From the experiences of many people in small groups, we have distilled the following guidelines for leaders.

What will be said is too brief to count as a course in leadership skills; and the nature of the group process—which of course has a lot to do with human nature—means that even expanding these hints by reading widely on this subject ahead of time can complement but can never substitute for attentive, sympathetic full-time commitment to the participants in the group during the workshop hours.

2. The Leader As Model Communicator

The ideal of working together so that communication between couples and other individuals within the group is enhanced can only be reached if the participants grasp what such communication requires of them. The leader should be thoroughly acquainted with communication skills—not so much to be able to list the rules as to serve as an effective example for everyone.

Fundamental to success is the *attitude* of the leader. Simply put, if the participant couples are to explore seriously their values in relation to a Christian understanding of marriage, they need leaders who are flexible and open to the values of various people. This may not be easy for Christian leaders or for participants who have strong and well thought-out convictions about what the Bible requires of us on this or that point. Such leaders and group members will be tempted to think of the goal of the workshop as getting all the participants to share their particular set of interpretations and values. Before long they may be lecturing or preaching to the group, slashing away with arguments or bludgeoning others with appeals to religious authority.

The alternative to that approach is *not* fuzzy-minded relativism, as though leaders are obliged to baptize just any opinion or value as Christian if it is held by a person who calls himself or herself a Christian. Certainly the leader's acceptance of the persons in the group and of their rights to their own values does not mean "agreeing with" all points of view. Asking the participants to accept others' opinions and values must never mean insisting that those participants give up their own convictions.

The effective leader will recognize that everyone's beliefs develop over a long period of time, under the influence of many people and circumstances. Since we are all finite and fallible human beings, we're all capable of blind spots, partial understandings, and downright mistaken beliefs. Even the apostle Paul claimed to see only "through a glass, darkly." With that sort of honesty serving as a check on the tendency to be dogmatic, and with a genuine expectation that the power of the Spirit of Christ will outdistance their meager and misguided zeal, leaders may develop (and this takes practice, too) an attitude of openness that will turn out to be far more effective as an agent of change in the life of participants than any calculated effort to preach or argue them out of their views.

What kinds of behavior will give expression to this openness and flexibility? One place where these are discussed at length is David Johnson's helpful *Reaching Out: Interpersonal Effectiveness and Self-Actualization* (Prentice-Hall, 1972), pages 61-83. Here we can mention only a few of the basic communication skills for small-group leaders seeking to build trust among participants:

—Responding to what is said with warmth, acceptance, and support;

—Engaging oneself in the self-disclosure sought in the participants;

—Giving understanding responses; for example, paraphrasing what someone has said in order to show this person that his or her remarks count in the discussion and to make sure that the point has come across to the group;

—Helping the discussion move forward by offering responses that will enable, or indeed oblige, a participant to clarify what he or she meant;

—Making personal ("I," "me," "my") and relationship ("I . . . you," "You . . . me," "We . . .") statements;

—Finding ways to confirm the strengths of the individual participants in one's responses;

—Monitoring the discussion by checking regularly with the participants to ascertain that effective communication is taking place.

There is one final point to make here about effective leadership; and it is so important for the success of building trust in the group that it should be made explicit to all the participants at the beginning of the workshop. Everyone taking part in the workshop must understand and respect the confidentiality of what goes on within the workshop. Opening oneself up to others is a special gift, and it must be received with care and mutual trust. Unless everyone knows and is committed to this guiding principle, the exchanges will be tense or superficial, and the potential of the group situation for mutual learning will go largely unrealized.

3. The Group Process

Understanding what is happening in group life and learning and achieving positive results is a fascinating and enriching experience for the leader. As we have suggested above, a good deal of the skill involved comes from the experience of working with different groups. With each new workshop the leader will gain more and more confidence in the group process itself. Couples who really care about each other can then begin to reach out more helpfully than other couples did in previous groups he led.

There are some typical stages on the way to this understanding which we can discuss here briefly, recognizing of course that each group is in many senses unique.

a. *Getting to know each other.* In a marriage preparation group the participants share a common purpose—learning about what makes for a happy married life. They will need time to develop a sense of trust and openness with each other. In most groups there will have to be a time of becoming acquainted, during which the participants learn a little about each other's background and experiences as a couple. Often it is useful during this period for each person to express his or her hopes of accomplishment during the workshop. One of the leaders may wish to make some written notes of the latter, checking later in the workshop to see whether these expectations are being addressed.

Already at this point in the workshop the effective leader will begin to sense the heterogeneity of the group members and will decide how to deal with them as unique individuals. Some couples may have more of the communications skills required for effective group participation than others. People like this may be ready for immediate openness themselves and become frustrated when others, less familiar with this kind of situation, hold back or resist. On the other hand, those who tend to be reticent may feel threatened by their fellow participants who are eager to plunge right into conversations about deeply personal matters.

The leaders must respect these differences. Patterns of discussion which reflect personal and relationship statements within the here-and-now of this group should be encouraged. It may be necessary to keep encouraging some couples so that they will share parts of their relationship, but it is unkind and unhelpful to push into an area of a person's or a couple's life when they have explicitly indicated that they are not ready to talk about it. As the leaders demonstrate listening with understanding and empathy and willingly open up part of their own lives, others will follow some of these patterns.

Getting acquainted is obviously necessary when some of the couples involved have had no previous contact with each other. Such a situation is likely to bring with it nervousness and uncertainty, but if dealt with properly, the absence of previously formed ideas about each other can be a strength. The leaders should acknowledge the problem of interaction between strangers at the outset, letting the group know that it will take some time for participants who were not previously acquainted to become comfortable with each other. It can be a rewarding experience indeed to watch a group of strangers begin to build trust and even friendships over the period of the workshop and to realize that some of the new friendships will become lasting relationships long after the workshop is over.

What may be less immediately evident is the need for couples who have known each other well prior to the workshop to "get acquainted." Such persons may find it difficult to get really involved in the sessions. During their previous relationships they may have systematically excluded sharing certain areas of life with each other, and they may thus be uncomfortable at the prospect of genuinely confronting these subjects when they arise in the course of the workshop. It is the alertness of the leaders to ways of moving beyond the set patterns these friendships have fallen into which is the key to success. Mixing up the group members during the get-acquainted period and in the other group exercises is an effective way to change these set patterns. In such situations humor can release a lot of anxiety. The leaders should continue to encourage couples to try out new behavior in the group and to stay in the here-and-now rather than falling back on the prior conventions of their friendships.

6. *Deciding what to do.* "Getting acquainted" continues throughout the workshop and beyond; it is not an activity that stops at a given point so that the group can move on to the next stage. But the period of "ice-breaking," as it is sometimes called, should not be drawn out too long. The amount of material to be covered in the workshop is substantial, and the group members will tackle it the more vigorously if they get a good start on the body of the work not too long after they get together.

A period of agenda-setting should begin soon, during which the couples take the opportunity to select areas of discussion they would particularly like to focus on. Naturally the group leaders will have an overall agenda related to the structure of the accompanying handbook, designed to help the couples explore the major elements of the marriage relationship.

The handbook distills the experience of many married couples to provide a digest of the most significant areas of importance in a relationship. Agenda-setting by the group insures that workshop time is apportioned in a way that will best meet the needs of all the participants. Structuring the workshop by the book alone or by the participants alone will be less effective than using the handbook to help organize the concerns each couple brings to the sessions and to insure that no important facets are ignored.

A word of caution should be stated about the use of structured exercises. At their best these will enable participants creatively to explore the most crucial sides of their relationships. There is a danger, however, that some people will be tempted to hide behind the exercises as a way of avoiding what they really need to talk about. Again, the leadership role is critical; alertness to this danger may indicate that participants have to be encouraged to keep in touch with their feelings and to express them. Of course, different groups will have differing norms for self-disclosure. Some will vary in the amount of self-disclosure that goes on at different points during the workshop.

c. *Moving through the work.* Once the agenda is set, the way the group handles it is critical. A general, perhaps even theoretical, discussion of career options, or sex roles, or child-rearing, or family relationships is far less helpful and important than seeing *how* couples discuss and deal with issues like these. An effective method is for one couple to allow the rest of the group to listen in on their interchange on a particular subject. One of the men, for instance, might begin telling the group how he sees his fiancée in her relationship to her parents. Through the encouragement of the leaders the dialogue may shift so that he is addressing her directly. The emotions surrounding the issue of the place of parents before and after marriage may emerge more clearly. The partners, in turn, will be able to practice genuine listening to each other.

During this interchange the group should not sit by as passive onlookers but should begin to identify with the couple, accepting and supporting both partners and responding in an understanding way. Different sorts of emotions may rise and wane in this sort of interchange; later we will have something to say about dealing with those emotions which do not tend to contribute constructively to the workshop.

In a weekend workshop the group will usually be moving at a steady and comfortable pace by late Saturday morning. Several couples will have had an opportunity to get into the discussion. Increasingly, participants will discover that some of the other group members are identifying with and supporting them, so they will risk getting into the more painful and uncertain aspects of their relationships with their partners. By Saturday afternoon, following a lunch break, the couples will be able to move smoothly through the afternoon agenda. When the dinner hour arrives, they will be amazed how far the group has progressed and how interesting a sustained workshop like this can be.

Experience has shown that a somewhat longer dinner break—two hours rather than one—will pay dividends in the evening session. Couples who have had time to relax and to reflect quietly together are often most comfortable on Saturday evening, which makes this a good time for discussing a very personal subject—sexual communication.

Sunday is a time for sharing what has been learned, consolidating some of the insights gained, identifying together the new skills which the group experience has taught, and talking together about some of the good and the bad patterns of relationships. A period of worship provides a chance for the group to celebrate together in gratitude to God for human love and for the divine love it reflects. Even when the structured agenda has been completed, new breakthroughs are possible. When all is said and done, the last day will prove for many to be the most important day of the session.[1]

The rhythm of a workshop where this handbook is used on two Saturdays or for a series of evening sessions, for example, will differ from that of an intensive, weekend schedule. The weekend model just described builds to a natural peak. When a week of everyday life intervenes between sessions, on the other hand, the leaders must find ways to compensate for the loss of momentum. Each session may have to start with a kind of "reentry" exercise to get the participants back into the spirit of the group atmosphere and once again get them feeling comfortable with each other. Even so, the leaders must accept the fact that some sessions will be more important to some of the individuals than to others; some may reach a high level of self-disclosure; others will be less intensive.

4. How People React in Groups (and What to Do About It)

The infinite variety of human personalities makes for one of the most enriching elements of small-group learning. Without differences between people life would be one-dimensional and dull. But orchestrating the variety of personalities that constitute the typical marriage preparation group to produce a harmonious learning experience instead of mere chaos and uproar taxes the imagination of the most experienced leader. Here are some brief and general hints for dealing with some common personality traits that may interfere with reaching the group's objectives.[2]

a. *The dominator.* Not long after the sessions begin you start to feel uneasy about what you first took to be this person's enthusiasm for plunging right in. It begins to seem as though this person not only wants to have the first and last

---

[1]Further exploration of group process and facilitative leadership in groups may be found in Carl Rogers, *Carl Rogers on Encounter Groups* (New York: Harper and Row, 1970), pp. 14-68.

[2]This section is modeled after some work done by a colleague of the author, L. Wayne Bryan, in an unpublished facilitators' manual at Drake University.

word on every subject but most of the words in between as well.

Tread cautiously here; you surely don't want to discourage participation in general. Perhaps at the end of the first session some feedback from the whole group about participation will sharpen the focus on the problem. Don't allow the group to deal too harshly with the dominator, though. If necessary, a private chat with this person during one of the breaks, enlisting his or her help in drawing out some of the more reticent group members, will ease the point across. It follows that the more the other members feel confident about participating, the less opportunity there will be for one person to dominate.

b. *The shy person.* The opposite problem can be just as frustrating and just as harmful to effective group process. What do you do about someone who volunteers nothing, answers questions in monosyllables, or even refuses to participate in an activity?

The first thing to remember is that it is neither kind nor effective to make the person feel bad about his or her level of participating. Encourage this person, but reassure him or her that the group will not pry or push. If the person chooses to sit out one of the planned activities, invite him or her to express how he or she feels about not participating in it—again, not in a way that would suggest that he or she is thereby ruining it for everyone else. Perhaps the feedback time at the end of the first session will help the person try out some new behavior. Here too, as with the dominator, a private consultation with this person by one of the leaders during a break may be beneficial.

c. *The storyteller.* We said earlier that humor is a great reliever of tension in group experiences. Besides, anecdotes, even jokes, can often teach lessons about life much more effectively than lectures, sermons, or arguments. Unfortunately, there are limits to their effectiveness, which some people do not recognize. For every point that is made this person will have a quip or a funny story; for every problem this person will be eager to report how he or she has dealt with it in the past.

Two things have to be conveyed gently but firmly to such a participant. First of all, the couples have come together for an intensive, learning experience. Not taking these sessions seriously enough is just as counterproductive as taking them too seriously. And secondly, the learning in the workshop depends to a very significant extent on the willingness and readiness of all participant couples to remain in the here-and-now. Continually reverting to past experiences works against that attitude.

d. *The irritable person.* Given the intensity of the discussion in a small group and the deeply personal nature of some of the subjects being discussed in a marriage readiness seminar, it is no wonder that feelings sometimes run high, with irritation or anger—whether with one's partner or with another group member—simmering to the surface. How does the leader handle conflict creatively so that relationships may be enhanced, not threatened, when sensitive subjects are discussed?

Denying or ignoring the feelings of anger or irritation in the hope that they will take care of themselves is bound to be disappointing. Instead, encourage people to practice effective, listening skills so that each person will genuinely hear what others are saying and feeling at points of disagreement.

e. *The philosopher.* Occasionally there is a participant in a group, often (but not always) someone well-educated, who will be expert at analyzing the issues in a profound, theoretical manner but who will resist mightily any personal involvement in the discussion. Such a person may even justify his or her abstract, impersonal approach as coming from high principles, claiming that the truth of the matter is more important than how anyone feels about it.

No doubt about it, the perceptive analyzer can contribute a great deal to the group by way of clarifying issues and questions. There are points at which a measure of detachment is extremely desirable for bringing out a real issue from a welter of irrelevant, emotional baggage. But the person who wants to focus only on "the truth of the matter" must be brought to recognize also that the revolutionary vitality of the biblical view of truth comes from the insistence that it has to become real in our lives. If we resist asking ourselves, "How does this truth apply to me?" and "How are these principles realized—made real—in my relationships with others?" our concern about truth will be misplaced. Persuading a person that such openness will enhance the value of the workshop for him or her will no doubt require the leader to appeal to the philosopher in the very logical line of thinking that creates the problem in the first place.

5. Facing Problems

We have implied throughout that the successful workshop will not necessarily be relaxed and comfortable at every moment. But those moments when tension looms must be dealt with creatively so that the result will be better understanding and communication. There are certain situations to which effective leaders should be particularly sensitive, for they represent the possibility of growth if handled properly. Again mindful of the limits of this brief introduction, here are some observations about these situations.

a. *Nonverbal signals.* Not everything we communicate comes across in words. The tone of a person's voice may communicate a whole range of different meanings while he or she uses the same words. An anxious appearance may betray the presence of worries which the person has not yet dared to articulate. Foot tapping, finger tapping, and staring off into space are obvious signs of boredom or distraction. Needless to say, leaders should not jump to hasty conclusions about this or that behavioral signal, particularly when dealing with persons with whom leaders may not be well acquainted. Many mannerisms are simply matters of habit. Still, sensitivity to and periodic checking of these nonverbal signals may be helpful and productive for the whole group.

b. *Tension.* There will be times when couples have difficulty discussing their relationships. The other members of the group will often feel awkward at this point, unsure of how to respond. Some will want to be reassuring; others will be inclined to change the subject. The skillful leader will keep the focus on the couple having difficulty in this situation. By offering some support and reinforcement to them for their willingness to open up the discussion at this point, leaders can help the partners stay in tune with each other. Listening empathically is often the most creative contribution the leaders and other group members can make. Similarly, should an individual become upset or burst into tears, he or she should be encouraged to express the feelings that have led to this response. Reassurance is very important. Put-downs and judgmental remarks about one person will threaten the entire group.

Occasionally a participant may have difficulty with a particular exercise and may react negatively to having to take part in it. Allow that person to ventilate those feelings, but allow others to express their reactions as well. Often the total pattern of responses to an exercise or episode in group life will give perspective to everyone, even the person with the negative feelings. When someone gets the impression that he or she does not have the right to express such feelings, that individual may be inclined to quit the group.

c. *Silence.* Periods of silence will occur in any group. Sometimes such a period will happen at the beginning of a session, even after the agenda is set. Silence comes with the ebb and flow of human thought and emotion. But though silence is proverbially said to be golden, for many people it is simply awkward. The leaders must recognize silence as an occasion for another kind of growth in the group.

Whether at the beginning of the session or after a particularly productive period of interaction, which has issued in the resolution of a key issue, silence offers a chance for the participants to tune into their own feelings, to let their concerns outside of the group fall away, and to concentrate on the central areas of their relationships with the other participants, especially their partners.

Some leaders, however, are afraid that silence indicates that they are unprepared for, or are inept at, the leadership task. Their temptation will be to break the silence immediately. In so doing, the potential of using silence for positive learning will be lost. Besides, the pattern of introducing new material instead of allowing for silence will lead the group to expect the leaders to be more responsible for continuing the flow of the workshop than they ought to be. The danger of this sort of leadership is that the couples are carried along without having a proper chance to register their own particular interests independently of the leaders' agenda.

6. Suggestions and Exercises

It's likely that the best leadership in a marriage preparation workshop comes when the couple who is leading are real and authentic as involved participants. Becoming involved is particularly helpful at points when the discussion is straying from the personal and interpersonal level. Then the leaders' account of their own experiences can serve to focus the discussion for the group. It will also increase the confidence of participants if they see that the leaders have a stake in the sharing and openness that they are calling on others to have.

Give everyone an opportunity to speak early in the workshop. For many people—maybe most—the most difficult contribution they make will be the first. Drawing out people in the first session will contribute to the success of the rest of the workshop.

While remaining conscious of the need not to get bogged down, encourage group members to express their feelings, whether positive or negative, for it is when this happens that the group begins to grow in trust. If a participant's observation is not acknowledged by others in the group, show appreciation for the comment and encourage others, particularly the partner of that person, to respond as well.

Remember that expertise in all of these techniques, honed in session after session, can never by itself substitute for deep concern for the participants and for sensitivity to their values, strengths and weaknesses, and needs. You are helping people prepare for a life together within the Christian community. That ought to be a joyful, rewarding experience, not a chore to get over with or a minefield to pick your way through.

What follows is an exercise that will present you with ten incidents arising in typical marriage preparation workshops. Each situation is created by a remark made by one member of one of the participating couples. Following this remark are four statements which a group facilitator might make in response. Rank these responses as you judge them to be—least helpful, which would be a (1), to most helpful, which would be a (4). When you have completed judging the ten situations, check your answers against those provided in the key at the end.

For further preparation go back to the statements and imagine what your response to the person's remark would be—whether it would be one of the four given or something entirely different. Remember that at this point in the process the goal is to help the participants tune into their own feelings, attitudes, and values before exploring solutions to the problems.

A further skill-building exercise follows, in which are explained different types of responses that may be appropriate in different situations.

1. Amy:

"My future mother-in-law is always putting David and me down. She acts as if we can't make our own decisions, and she keeps asking David—behind my back—about my family and background. You know, it's really none of her business. I wish she'd just leave us alone."

Responses:

A. _____ It's really strange that you feel that way about your future mother-in-law. You'd better get things straightened out, or you'll have more trouble later on.

B. _____ David's mother is probably just as concerned as you are about you and David having a good marriage. You know, Amy, she may be threatened by your relationship with David.

C. _____ You're really bothered by the way your mother-in-law-to-be is relating to you, and you feel as if she's treating you and David as though you weren't young adults at all.

D. _____ How close has David's mother been to him? How accustomed has David been to her help in making important decisions for him?

2. George:

"Judy clams up every time we get into a disagreement! She won't look at the problem and work out a solution; instead, she keeps saying I don't understand how she feels. How *can* I understand if we can't talk about the problem together?"

Responses:

A. _____ I'm sure that the longer you and Judy are together the more you'll understand each other's feelings. It's just a matter of getting used to each other.

B. _____ It sounds as if you're getting frustrated, George, with not being able to find an effective way for you and Judy to work through differences, especially when you're not certain about her real feelings on an issue.

C. _____ Your problem seems to be one of wanting to find solutions to problems without first communicating to Judy that you really understand how she feels about the problem.

D. _____ I wonder what's behind Judy's reluctance to talk about a disagreement? How do you try to get her to express her feelings during a conflict?

3. Jim:

"I really can't see that much difference between Sue's religion and mine. In her church they use 'trespasses' in the Lord's Prayer and in ours we use 'debts.' So what's the difference? I think she's more religious than I am, but I'm certainly open to her doing what she wants as far as church is concerned."

Responses:

A. _____ It seems as if you and Sue have some different values concerning the practice of your religious faith; and you might have some conflicts here if Sue expects to have more participation in church life than you anticipate for yourself.

B. _____ It's good that you and Sue can be open with each other about your religious life style, Jim, but you certainly seem to be playing down the most important area for building a solid marriage.

C. _____ I sense that you share a common, religious background, which should be a plus in making future decisions.

D. _____ You see some similarities in your religious backgrounds, but you also see some differences between yourself and Sue in the present meaning of church life and church activities in your life styles.

4. Nancy:

"Tim and I are really pleased with the way we can take the time to review together the day's events after we both get through with work or school, to talk about both good and bad experiences. We're learning to listen to each other and to understand what the little things are that please or distress each of us."

Responses:

A. _____ It really sounds as though the two of you are making some great progress at tuning in to each other.

B. _____ What is each of you finding out about your partner's likes and dislikes?

C. _____ So you're really finding a mutually satisfying way of sharing your lives with each other.

D. _____ I'm glad to hear that you're able to talk together. I hope that you will soon learn to pray together.

5. Marcia:

"I really don't think Bob fights fairly. He acts as if he always has the superior reasoning—like I'm just stupid and don't have any good sense about anything. He's always Mr. Right. I get so mad at him at times. He just smiles back, and that makes it even worse!"

Responses:

A. _____ If I were you, Marcia, I wouldn't get too upset about that. Remember that we as Christians have to be patient with each other.

B. _____ I wonder if the two of you, instead of listening to each other, just assume that you're going to have different points of view whenever there's a touch of conflict.

C. _____ Let's take a few minutes to explore the issues you argue or disagree about the most, and then let's look at the ways you talk to each other.

D. _____ You're feeling as if Bob doesn't really take you seriously when you have a conflict but rather makes you feel like a little girl who doesn't know quite enough.

6. Randy:

"Sally and I have decided we want to wait to begin a family until we have some time to build our marriage relationship and some financial security. We differ about how long we'll wait, but neither of us is eager to have children for at least two years. She wants four kids; I think two is plenty."

Responses:

A. _____ Well, I think you're right to wait till you get to know each other well.

B. _____ What criteria are each of you using to determine how many kids you want?

C. _____ It sounds as if you have some common agreement about building your own relationship before you launch into being parents, but it looks as if you still have some differences about family size to resolve.

D. _____ You say you agree about strengthening your relationship before having a family, but you seem to be putting off dealing with your differences on family size.

7. Fern:

"I'm really wondering if Max knows how best to help me when I've got a tough decision to make. He comes up with answers *for* me, but I'm not sure that's what I need."

Responses:

A. _____ So Max comes up with answers before you're sure what the factors surrounding the decisions really are.

B. _____ You're wondering how Max might be most helpful to you when you're struggling with a decision, but you're not sure the best way to help you is for him to provide solutions to the problem?

C. _____ Rather than get too upset, Fern, don't you think you're lucky that Max tries to help you with your decisions?

D. _____ You don't need to get so upset, really. This is a problem now, but I'm sure you and Max will work it out.

8. Rick:

"Well, our biggest question right now centers around Mary's attitudes toward making love. We're committed to each other, and I feel that we should be able to express our love fully, but she feels that we should hold back until after the wedding ceremony. I think that's really limiting our relationship!"

Responses:

A. _____ Maybe there are some good reasons for you to consider Mary's point of view.

B. _____ What do you sense are Mary's reasons for holding back, Rick?

C. _____ You're feeling that Mary's reasons for holding back are hang-ups from the past?

D. _____ You feel committed to Mary and you want to express your love sexually, but you find Mary's reluctance to be a barrier to further closeness.

9. Jason:

"Peggy and I have examined our career interests, and we've decided that she'll work full time until we decide to have children. Then she won't work again until the kids are in school. I believe a mother should stay at home as long as the children are at home."

Responses:

A. _____ You feel strongly that you should be the breadwinner in the family, Jason, and that your wife should take a traditional mother role, with her career interests being secondary.

B. _____ You and Peggy have worked through your career and parental values, and you've agreed that Peggy would give priority to an at-home mother role, with her career interests being of secondary importance during the child-bearing time.

C. _____ Jason, you talk about you and Peggy agreeing on your parental decisions, but it sounds as if your own opinions really decided the matter.

D. _____ On what basis did you and Peggy make your career and parental decisions?

10. Laura:

"Tommy and I have different feelings about the use of our money. I think we ought to be saving our money for furniture, but he keeps putting money into his car. I know it's not officially 'our' money, but we've got to start planning now. I'm worried we won't be able to agree later on in this area."

Responses:

A. _____ Laura, you and Tommy had better sit down right away and decide how much of your budget will be used in different areas during the first year of your marriage.

B. _____ Don't be too worried about it, Laura. It'll take time for you and Tommy to learn to share your resources and make wise decisions, but you'll learn to think about each other's needs and interests.

C. _____ You're finding in this area of finances in your relationship that you and Tommy have some different values and that you expect some real conflict when you begin to pool your financial resources.

D. _____ My hunch is that both you and Tommy are reflecting the financial values of your parents, Laura. I'll bet you haven't talked much with each other about the management and use of your income.

Key:

1.	A-1	B-2	C-4	D-3	6.	A-1	B-3	C-4	D-2
2.	A-1	B-4	C-2	D-3	7.	A-3	B-4	C-1	D-2
3.	A-3	B-1	C-2	D-4	8.	A-1	B-3	C-2	D-4
4.	A-3	B-2	C-4	D-1	9.	A-3	B-4	C-1	D-2
5.	A-1	B-2	C-3	D-4	10.	A-1	B-2	C-4	D-3

In any given situation the helping person (receiver) may make one of five different types of responses to what the person being helped (sender) says.

(E) *Evaluative:* This is a response which indicates that the receiver is making a judgment of the goodness, appropriateness, effectiveness, or rightness of the sender's problem.

In some way the receiver is implying what the sender ought to do or might do.

(I) *Interpretative:* This response indicates that the receiver intends to teach the sender what his or her problem means, how he or she *really* feels about the situation. Either obviously or subtly the receiver implies what the sender might think or ought to think about the problem.

(S) *Supportive:* With a supportive response the receiver is reassuring or pacifying the sender or reducing the intensity of his or her feeling. The receiver has in some way implied that the sender need not feel as he or she does.

(P) *Probing:* With a probing response the receiver intends to seek further information, provoke further discussion along a certain line, or question the sender. In some way the receiver has implied that the sender ought to discuss—or might profitably discuss—a certain point further.

(U) *Understanding:* This response is merely an effort to ask the sender whether or not the receiver has correctly understood what the sender is saying, how the sender feels about the problem, and how the sender sees the problem.[3]

In the key to the exercise about the ten incidents just completed, a (1), or least helpful, was assigned to evaluative responses. Supportive and interpretative responses usually earned a (2). Probing responses were usually given a (3). Understanding responses received a (4), or most helpful.

Mark well that most types of responses can be quite appropriate at different times in the process of listening and responding, though it is seldom the case that an unsolicited, evaluative response is very helpful at the initial stage of interacting together. At that point it is mostly understanding that the sender needs so that he or she can proceed further with confidence. Early interpretation or probing is really short-circuiting the process, and the results may be confusing,

---

[3]David W. Johnson, *Reaching Out: Interpersonal Effectiveness and Self-Actualization.* (Englewood Cliffs, N.J.: Prentice-Hall, Inc., 1972), p. 125. Used by permission.

inhibiting, or frustrating for the sender, no matter how good the intention of the helping person.

Using the remarks and responses above, mark each one as *E, I, S, P,* or *U,* according to types of responses described above. The key follows.

	A	*B*	*C*	*D*
1.	E	I	U	P
2.	S	U	I	P
3.	I	E	S	U
4.	S	P	U	E
5.	E	I	P	U
6.	E	P	U	I
7.	I	U	E	S
8.	E	P	I	U
9.	I	U	E	P
10.	E	S	U	I

CHAPTER
2

Workshop
Overview

Workshop Overview

It's important to be realistic about what can actually be achieved in a single forty-eight-hour workshop.

Very general objectives, ranging across many issues which affect interpersonal relationships and particularly marriage, are offered in the following "Workshop Overview." Sensitive leaders will, of course, vary their styles, their models, and especially their specific objectives to fit the couples with whom, and for whom, the workshop is sponsored. As a result the workshop itself will yield different results (by design as well as by accident) each time it is conducted.

But we mustn't forget that the entire workshop and each session within it are designed to achieve *something*. Each workshop is not going to result in 100 percent changed lives, but surely some change in the form of discovery, learning, and application ought to occur.

It's tempting to get caught up in the process of a workshop; then it becomes easy to lose sight of the goals. When that happens, it becomes dangerously likely that—even if the weekend itself is a pleasurable event—there will be little long-term benefit for the participants.

Objective One: Family Background

One of the most important parts of personal growth is recognizing the impact that family background and personal history have on one's choices and life style. Many couples tend to view differences in social class and socioeconomic background as of little importance in determining marital happiness.

Not until two years into the marriage did Harry realize that his wife, Betty, was determined to spend two weeks at home with her mother *every* summer, immersing herself in some volunteer project, which had been her family tradition for decades. Suddenly Harry began to wonder if Betty could really break those close emotional ties with her family in order to build her own family.

For the workshop described in this manual one objective is to help couples at least begin to understand the family backgrounds from which they come and the influence of those backgrounds on partner selection and compatibility. Attention will also be given to changing relationships when couples become parents and the role expectations of couples in their new relationship.

Objective Two: Communication Patterns

It has been said that a married couple "cannot *not* communicate." That's probably true, but the more important issue is whether their communication patterns are constructive or destructive. Interpersonal interaction can bring two people closer together; it can also cause them to move further apart. Often it does neither but simply leaves both people where they were in the first place.

The effects of communication are generally directly related to the level at which that communication occurs.

Most of our conversations occur at level one and consist of little more than *casual communication*. We discuss the weather, talk about sports, and pass along the latest jokes and gossip. In casual communication our ears and our mouths are involved, but our *selves* are kept out of the conversation.

At level two we engage in *personal communication*. We talk about and listen with interest while others talk about issues which are important to both speaker and listeners: children, mates, parents, plans, finances, illnesses, friends, and so forth. As we have casual communication (level one) with an acquaintance, so we have personal communication (level two) with our friends.

But there is also a third level which is important to most people. At this level we experience *intimate communication.* Intimacy allows us to disclose our fears and our secret dreams, to risk others' images of ourselves by letting them know us deeply, and to respond gently and respectfully when another person reveals himself or herself to us.

At all levels communication is more than merely verbal. For example, a handshake might be appropriate to casual communication, a hug to personal communication, and sexual intercourse to intimate communication. We communicate best when we communicate completely—with our eyes, hands, and ears, as well as our mouths.

An important objective for this workshop is to help couples recognize and practice good communication, especially at levels two and three, and to encourage couples to seek intimate communication in their marriages.

Objective Three: Spirituality

Del and Trudy Vander Haar have integrated their Christian understanding of relationships throughout their personal statement of their own marriage (chapter 3, "A Personal Experience"). One goal for this workshop is to help couples, through various activities in the workshop, find spiritual meaning and vitality in the entire range of their relationship, from supportive listening strategies to sexual intimacy.

A common concern is to help couples realize that spirituality must characterize their whole life together, not merely during Sunday mornings. The "Theological Reflection" which accompanies Session 3 (Description and Log in chapter 5) can be helpful in this regard.

At the same time couples need to look specifically at the

way worship, prayer, and other acts of piety can enrich the rest of their relationship. Expectations for participation in church life and family nurturing patterns may vary greatly between couples in the workshop. Some models for spiritual growth in the lives of couples and in family life will be introduced. Couples will be challenged to begin thinking of their marriage ceremony as a covenantal event so that their lives can be later lived in covenant faithfulness.

Objective Four: Coping Strategies for Conflict Within Marriage

Many couples are successful at avoiding direct dealing with conflict before marriage. When conflicts arise, partners often set up a complete avoidance pattern, hoping the disagreement will work itself out through the affection and the good will which lovers demonstrate toward each other.

Because of the sense of trust and openness possible in a marriage preparation group, individual partners will risk opening up areas of interpersonal conflict or discomfort. If couples can gain some skill in handling potentially disputative interaction nondefensively, they will learn to gain a greater intimacy through periods of stress, and they may even come to anticipate times of conflict within marriage as times for potential growth. That, at least, is one goal.

Objective Five: "Nonagenda Agenda"

An important part of a weekend workshop is group time that is not assigned a predesignated focus but is nevertheless maintained as an essential session.

In the security of a workshop setting issues are constantly being introduced, and couples are being helped to grapple with those issues. But the couples also came into the workshop carrying their own issues, their own concerns (or "agendas"). Some time in the workshop must be given to help couples with their own concerns—using the resources and the security of the group setting.

In this way the workshop can have another goal: to help couples identify and discuss issues not specifically raised, or not resolved, in the preplanned workshop sessions.

Objective Six: Parenthood Decisions

Using the communication and value clarification skills learned early in the workshop, couples are encouraged in a later session to freely explore their attitudes about becoming parents.

We live in a time when some couples are deliberately choosing the option of remaining childless, while others are delaying parenthood until both partners become established in careers. For Christians parenthood decisions may be particularly difficult because there appear to be competing claims on their values.

Though this issue may initially seem to be in the distant future for some couples, it is very important for each person to know what his or her partner expects regarding parenthood *before* marriage. One goal of this workshop is for couples to be motivated (and provided a model) to make joint decisions regarding parenthood.

Objective Seven: Sexual Intimacy

In an age of open and candid exploration of sexual values, the workshop leader may wrongly assume that most couples are well equipped to build a healthy sexual relationship. Though young people are usually embarrassed to admit it, many still lack a basic understanding of the emotional and physical aspects of sexual love, especially where individual needs are concerned.

During this workshop couples will review attitudes and ideas which helped shape their own views on sexuality, and they will look at concerns and hopes for sexual fulfillment in their marriages. One goal is that couples will be able to discuss sexuality without anxiety and will value the importance of sexuality in marriage.

Objective Eight: Goal Setting and Financial Planning

Though the parental session may touch on some financial and career issues, couples need time to fully explore both a goal-setting process and the mutual goals they'd like to set in these matters. Career and financial goals are treated together in this workshop, because couples experience them as related concerns.

Where do we go with our dreams? What does career fulfillment mean to all of us? What kind of financial pattern do we anticipate in the next five years? How will we make decisions about money and manage the day-to-day financial accounts?

The objective here is to help couples anticipate some of their immediate and financial patterns. Further financial and problem-solving resources are also available (see chapter 7, "Additional Resources").

Objective Nine: Where Do We Go From Here?

As the weekend concludes, opportunity will be given for couples to summarize their learnings and to identify some functional goals they can implement in the immediate future.

Learning involves changes in behavior, and changes in behavior do not happen without planning and reinforcement and follow-up.

A time of celebration as a Christian community of couples will conclude the workshop. The experience of our life together during the workshop will form a natural context for our lifting each other up toward the grace of God.

A Postscript:

There are so many myths about marriage ("They lived happily ever after." . . . "The domestic grind." . . . "Is that all there is?" . . . "Another sucker falls.") that many young people today are genuinely confused or uncertain about risking marriage. The focus of this workshop centers on the "here-and-now" of the couples' relationships. If some effective communication and trust patterns can occur in the present, then partners are more likely to face struggles and challenges in the future with greater confidence and creativity, and with less fear of myths.

And though it's difficult to anticipate the future with realistic planning in an ever-changing culture and economy, the scope of the workshop is designed to help couples at least consider central issues for living together as married couples. Strong *lead couples* (who have satisfying, growing, imperfect marriages) will help young couples see some good, realistic models for learning effective communication and decision making.

The workshop's focus on realistic expectations is intended as neither a scare tactic nor an antidote to romance; rather, it should instill a healthy sense of human experience. Marriage can only be fulfilling when we, by the grace of God, learn how to love each other in the day-to-day ordinariness of our lives.

CHAPTER
3

A Personal
Experience

CHAPTER 3

A Personal Experience

Del and Trudy Vander Haar had led many Marriage Enrichment Seminars before their son, Tim, made plans to get married. What follows are some excerpts from a booklet these parents wrote for their son and future daughter-in-law for their preparation for marriage. It conveys some of the special expertise that comes from counseling dozens of couples, to be sure, but even more it shares insights and wisdom gained from nearly thirty years of working together at a marriage of their own.

*　　*　　*

Someone once said that "getting married is a simple act . . . but becoming partners in a caring relationship is a lifelong challenge." That sounds obvious and profound at the same time. Unfortunately statistics would seem to indicate that most married couples today are learning this truth the hard way—a way so hard that many of them haven't the will to keep at it.

Once it was social pressure that held a lot of shaky marriages together. So darkly did the community frown on divorce that many people endured years of strife-torn and loveless marriages for appearance' sake. In today's social climate, however, divorce has become much easier to obtain than in earlier years, which means that the motivation for tolerating and enduring an unhappy marriage is more difficult to come by than it was then.

Difficult, but not impossible. And to succeed at a marriage, to develop the internal cohesion that will hold two people together in the absence of external coercion, is a tremendously satisfying accomplishment for both. The New Testament, you recall, uses the relationship of Christ's love for the church as a model for the relationship of husband and wife. That's quite a goal to strive for.

Intimacy is a word we hear tossed around a great deal these days. It's an important part of a happy marriage. But one of the secrets of finding intimacy is that we don't go looking for it. What we have to do is lose ourselves in the other person. When we lose ourselves in someone else, we find ourselves, and we achieve true intimacy with that person.

In the early part of this century a man named Edward Carpenter wrote a book called *Love's Coming of Age*. We like his description of intimacy, even if it does sound a little old-fashioned to contemporary ears:

> That there should exist one other person in the world toward whom all openness of interchange should establish itself, from whom there should be no concealment; whose body should be as dear to one, in every part, as one's own; with whom there should be no sense of Mine or Thine, in property or possession; into whose mind one's thoughts should naturally flow, as it were to know themselves and to receive a new illumination; and between whom and oneself there should be a spontaneous rebound of sympathy in all the joys and sorrows and experiences of life; such is perhaps one of the dearest wishes of the soul.

But don't ever imagine that that kind of intimacy just happens to people who live together long enough. Married people achieve a close relationship by a process we might call *mutual adaptation*. Listen to David and Vera Mace's clever illustration of it:

Imagine a group of porcupines settling down to sleep on a cold winter night. Being warm-blooded creatures, they huddle together in search of mutual warmth. But the point inevitably is reached when sharp quills prick tender flesh, and they recoil away from each other. In this fashion they shuffle sleepily back and forth, back and forth, until they find a point of equilibrium at which they derive the maximum possible amount of warmth from each other, consistent with not pricking each other!

If partners in a good marriage work at that adaptation to each other, we think they become a little bit more than they were by themselves. That's happened to each of us in almost three decades together. We've both continued to grow. Relationships are never static. Every living thing is either growing or dying. And marriage is for *life!*

*   *   *

It took us a long time to get to the point of sharing our feelings with each other and being sensitive to what the other person was feeling. Your dad was not accustomed to identifying— much less sharing—his feelings under pressure, which led your mother to suppose that her husband was always self-sufficient and never needed building up. It was a little unsettling to her romantic idealism to discover that the man she married was not exactly the unflappable Rock of Gibraltar she had thought; it was equally unsettling for your father, with his well-entrenched image of the male role to be never admitting weakness, to open up and share some of his insecurities.

We've really been helped by discovering and identifying various levels of communication and becoming aware of these when we have talked to each other. Different writers have given different names to the levels; we've found these four words useful:

> friendly
> blaming
> informing
> feeling

ou can move from one of these levels to another, con-
ıously and freely, you'll be provided new opportunities for
ıntimacy.

*   *   *

Not that there aren't any struggles!

Conflict is natural and inevitable. The closer our lives are
meshed, the more there is to fight about. Here is where the
romantic myth can really wreak havoc. We remember an old
friend who married a dashing, adventuresome man she met
on a round-the-world cruise. Back home she was soon com-
plaining bitterly to us about their differing goals—which she
could have figured out before marriage—and the fact that he
was no longer as romantic as he used to be. Doing a little
clear-headed thinking before rushing to the altar—in place of
misty-eyed wishing—could have spared her a lot of anxiety.
Worse yet, she then gave up on the marriage almost immediately. When a couple of people care enough, they are
willing to work at differences. Resolving differences is a
greater—and usually more difficult—evidence of maturity
than is throwing in the towel.

Charlie Shedd remarks that the difference between the
ass and the donkey is that when danger threatens donkeys,
they put their heads together and kick outward but when
danger threatens asses, they put their backsides together and
kick each other. Problems are bound to come. The important
difference is whether you kick the problem or each other.

We don't mean to suggest that you can entirely avoid the
threat of getting angry with each other. Anger is one of many
ways people handle conflicts between them. Dr. Mace says
that anger is an involuntary emotion that serves to protect us
from our enemies, but he goes on to remind us that husbands
and wives are not enemies!

So how do people release tension? Your mother tends to
be verbal, reacting quickly with a sharp wit and a sharp tongue.
Your father has a much slower fuse and perhaps is more
physical than verbal—but fortunately he doesn't get angry

very often. From talking to many couples, we'd agree that the most commonly destructive way of handling conflict is neither verbal nor physical but the silent treatment. Almost as hurtful are reactions like constantly dredging up old offenses, resorting to the old dig, "You're just like your mother (or father)," or forever inflicting just a little bit more retribution for a fault of long ago.

Most of all, it's important to clarify what the conflict is really about. That takes time, but it's time well spent if it avoids conflict over a misunderstanding. Some conflicts center on things that just aren't worth fussing about. Here's a simple example: Your mother learned from her mother a recipe for salmon loaf that she tried for years to feed to your father, who can appreciate salmon fishing as a sport but has absolutely no use for the canned salmon that was the basic ingredient in this particular recipe. For your mother, though, salmon loaf was virtually a family tradition. Did life ever become simpler when we stopped struggling and just eliminated salmon loaf from our menus!

At deeper levels, of course, it's even more important for husbands and wives not to try to make each other over and learn instead to love and accept each other as they are. Nobody likes to be nagged. The tricky thing to decide is what things are worth the effort to change and what things really don't make any difference as they are. The maturity to accept feedback from your mate is much more easily acquired if you realize that he or she is really thinking of your happiness, not his or her selfish concerns. You'll be amazed together at how often change takes place when the pressure to change is off.

*   *   *

How wonderful that God made each of us different! All of us have different skills, talents, personalities. A wise couple will take advantage of this diversity and not get into conflict over roles. This seems to come up at every marriage preparation seminar we conduct, particularly in the last few years when there's been much attention given to the whole question of role differences between men and women.

Maybe you remember a children's story called "Posh and Tosh," always a favorite in our house. Axel and Hannah were a peasant husband and wife who, after a lot of grousing at each other, traded places for one day. Hannah didn't seem to do all that badly in the fields, but poor Axel! The pig came into the house, the churn full of cream turned over, and the cow, which was tied to Axel's waist while it grazed, fell off the roof and pulled him up the chimney.

Probably what this quaint, old story is telling us is that rather than belittle the other person's role, we should help each other wherever we can.

That will take some experimenting. Many couples start out with one person taking care of the finances but switch somewhere along the line. What's important is keeping flexible and aware of each other's talents, skills, and interests.

Today a major consideration for an increasing number of married couples is who is to be the breadwinner and who the housekeeper. In many—perhaps most—cases it will end up that both will be partly both. It's a challenge to be willing to accept changing roles and to support each other in them. There'll be a lot of give-and-take in this area of roles. As in every other area success revolves around whether the two of you are a team or just a couple of people living together for convenience's sake. Each of us has his or her separate and interchangeable roles, but they should always be subordinate to our common goals.

*   *   *

We've sometimes drawn circles to illustrate the complicated process of merging two systems that goes on in a marriage. We start out like this:

Some couples never get any closer than this:

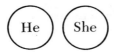

There may be some liberated people who like that kind of relationship. Others, by contrast, grow to be like this:

We think the ideal lies somewhere between those last two, probably something like this:

      As we said before, 1 + 1 = 3

A friend of ours was married to a husband so jealous and possessive of her that he had squeezed too hard, and there was nothing left. He didn't even allow her room to breathe while he insisted on being himself to such an extreme that he only put in an appearance when he felt like it. He finally gained his "freedom" through divorce—but that's not a very liberating kind of freedom, especially since he's always behind in his support payments.

This was an extreme case of neglect and abuse, but it can serve to remind us that freedom isn't freedom when it comes at the cost of hurting anyone else. Kahlil Gibran says in *The Prophet:*

Let there be spaces in your togetherness,
. . . .
And stand together yet not too near together:
For the pillars of the temple stand apart,
And the oak tree and the cypress grow not in each other's
shadow.

*   *   *

"For the love of money is the root of all evil," the Bible
tells us. From time immemorial, money has been a problem
for those who have it and for those who don't.

Christian teaching has much to say about money—in particular, that the person who serves money can't serve God
too. Money has to be a servant, not a master, something with
which we serve others and serve the Lord.

In the last few years many Christian people have become
more and more sensitive to the great imbalances in the way
the wealth of the world is distributed. They have come to see
that for Christians in our society it is often the same mate-
rialistic standards that determine their life styles as for those
who make no profession of following the One who asked what
profit there is to gaining the whole world if you lose your own
soul. It's important for couples to talk together about steward-
ship, about the responsibilities they have that extend beyond
the walls of their own home—responsibilities involving their
resources.

Even so, decisions about the use of money in your family
are going to arise every day. Those who have studied the
reasons marriages break up say that money is among the top
three causes. Within your overall decisions about life style—
and every couple planning marriage has to have a basic understanding about that—countless little decisions about spending
or not spending will have to be made.

Some couples decide to have separate bank accounts.
We've always felt it was wise to have a joint account, with a
budgeting system, so that there isn't "his" and "hers" money.
Like many other features of married life, earning, spending,

saving, and giving can be marvelous opportunities to work and to grow together, or they can constitute a stressful and divisive threat. We pray that you'll recognize the pitfalls and grasp the opportunities.

*   *   *

Many so-called marriage manuals these days devote almost all of their attention to sexual technique and performance. There's a lot of helpful information to be found in those manuals; in sex as in most other areas of life ignorance is *not* bliss. But in those manuals there's a lot of shoddy and selfish thinking, too, premised on the notion that the fundamental reality of the human race is biological. We hope that you'll be able to sift the helpful from the purely hedonistic.

We're not going to try to enumerate a lot of quick hints in this short space. In an advice column we recently read, "If there's harmony in the bedroom, usually there's harmony in the rest of the house." We'd like to turn that sentence around to emphasize the truth: "If there's disharmony in the rest of the house, there can't be harmony in the bedroom." If a husband and wife are not giving themselves to each other the rest of the time, they won't very long be able to give themselves to each other in bed.

Don't take sex *too* seriously. When people try too hard to satisfy their own sexual desires, they don't succeed at it. Trying to give pleasure to your partner is far more rewarding. It's good to have some of the child-at-play in us. We celebrate sex with joy because it's God's gift of making two people who really love each other one.

*   *   *

As Christians we believe that Christ enables us to act out our love for each other, taking away our natural selfishness, enabling us to be more willing to give to each other rather than to receive, and giving us the grace to forgive over and over again. There is probably no better guide for practicing love than what Paul wrote in 1 Corinthians 13. Read those verses often during your life together; measure yourself honestly against those standards; celebrate your growth together. Forgive each other—and yourself—when you haven't been patient or kind, when you've allowed envy or boasting or arrogance or rudeness to put yourself above your partner; when you've secretly or not so secretly relished the mistakes of your partner, and when you've been intolerant or unbelieving or hopeless or have given up.

God bless both of you as He's blessed us!

CHAPTER
4

Model for
a Weekend
Workshop

CHAPTER **4**

Model for a
Weekend Workshop

A *weekend* workshop has been selected as the most appropriate setting for a number of reasons.

After experimenting for several years with both weekend and weekly personal growth educational models, the author found that participants were able to maintain a higher level of personal and group involvement in an intensive weekend than in weekly sessions.

The weekend experience involves two nights that offer time needed for integration and reflection, without losing the momentum of the group. During the breaks couples have time for precessing what happened in the group and for making new discoveries outside the group. The continuity maintained keeps couples talking about their relationship even when they do not find enough group time for exploring everything. Weekly programs of premarriage education may, or may not, stimulate continuing couple dialogue of this sort.

Couples are actually together in the weekend group for approximately twenty *contact hours;* this is sufficient time for group life to develop and for each couple to have group time to focus on their own relationship.

If a church chooses a weekly program or other time-separated model as most suitable for a local situation, it will be important to build in reentry exercises at the beginning of each session so that couples will be able to relate to each other comfortably again after being separated from each other.

A very practical reason for weekend scheduling is the availability of participants. Not all potential marriage partners are living in the same community, and some may have to come a great distance for the workshop.

An alternative weekend model covering two Sunday afternoons (five hours each) is available from the Reverend Stanley Vugteveen, Minister of Family Life and Nurture, Emmanuel Reformed Church, Paramount, California 90723.

1. Preparing for the weekend

a. *Participants.* Participants for the workshop may be selected in a number of ways. Some churches make a marriage preparation workshop a required part of the premarital preparation process. Others approach this programing on a voluntary basis. Larger churches with steady groups of couples interested in marriage may wish to offer the workshop periodically as a part of the education program of the congregation. Other congregations will find that contracting with a cluster of churches in the community for a joint marriage preparation program will be most effective for their situation.

Whatever approach is taken, such a program will be helpful both for couples already engaged and for couples who are seriously contemplating marriage. Such a workshop could provide the help some couples need before they make (or decide not to make) a serious commitment to one another.

b. *Registration.* In registering participants, it is important that participants understand the time commitment to the entire experience. It's disruptive to the rest of the participants (as well as the learning process) to allow individuals to attend only part of the workshop. If both partners cannot be present for the entire experience, they should make arrangements for another workshop even if it means some inconvenience to the couple.

It's also important that each partner is sent a note that acknowledges registration and includes any preworkshop materials. In our culture it's usually the female partner who initiates contact with the pastor for a workshop of this kind. Though the male partner sometimes resists getting involved and may genuinely doubt the value of this experience, a personal letter to him as well as his partner may help build a good relationship with the pastor and enhance expectations for the weekend.

    c. *Leadership.* Continuity in leadership is essential. If the leader is a pastor, either a pastor on the church's staff or a pastor representing a cluster of churches is needed to assure continuity. Sometimes husband-wife ministry teams have had effective marriage enrichment training and would be available to a group of churches. Whatever leadership a church selects, the leader(s) ought to be experienced in marriage enrichment and group dynamics skills.

    Increasingly, lay couples are becoming part of such movements as the Association of Couples for Marriage Enrichment (ACME) and are eager to serve in a *lead couple* capacity. The lead couple(s) bring a sense of experience and reality testing to the workshop. They also provide invaluable help to the workshop facilitator. They may recognize needed group direction or give attention to couples who stay on the perimeter of the group. It's also very helpful (if possible) to have both a male and a female in the leadership role. A facilitator of the opposite sex often is able to understand and influence male-female dynamics in a most complementary way.

    d. *Preworkshop Inventory.* It's important that couples have some sense of what will be expected of them beyond attendance and participation. The following approach is recommended.

    Two weeks prior to the weekend send a copy of *The Marriage Expectation Inventory* (see chapter 5, "Participants' Materials") to each participant, asking that each participant meet with his or her partner for a two-hour block of time prior to the workshop to follow the directions given in the *Inven-*

tory. As the couple discusses their similarities and differ-ences, those issues that are not yet resolved should be circled for further exploration during the weekend (if the couple so desires). Consider a mailing similar to the following:

Dear _____ .

We are looking forward to your joining us for the Mar-riage Preparation Weekend, _____ (date). Many couples have found these weekends to be just the thing they needed to grow in their understanding of each other and to increase their ability to communicate with and care for each other.

What you get out of the weekend will depend largely on how much of yourself you put into the experience. We will be together as a group of couples for most of the weekend, learn-ing from each other and having some time alone. Direction will be given by the leaders, but sharing your own experiences will be a significant part of how we learn. That means some honesty and candor on your part will be necessary—but not in any forced or pushy way from the leaders.

A *Marriage Expectation Inventory* is enclosed to help you prepare for the weekend. Please plan to complete the *Inven-tory* before you arrive on Friday night, expecially noting those areas that need further discussion. A tentative schedule is also enclosed.

As you know, we think it's especially important that everyone be with us for *the entire weekend.*

We're anticipating a great time together!

With warm regards,

―――――――――――

2. Managing the Schedule
MARRIAGE PREPARATION WORKSHOP

FRIDAY NIGHT: *Session 1: Roles and Expectations*
   7:30– 8:15 *Getting Acquainted and Building the Group*
   8:15– 8:30 *Clarifying the Agenda*
   8:30– 8:45 BREAK
   8:45– 9:00 *Introduction of Description and Log*

9:00–10:00 *Role Expectation Inventory*
10:00–10:15 *Closing: Tuning in—Worship*

SATURDAY MORNING, AFTERNOON, EVENING:
  9:00–10:30 *Session 2: Communication*
10:30–10:45 BREAK
10:45–12:00 *Session 3: Spirituality*
12:00– 1:00 LUNCH
 1:00– 3:00 *Session 4: Conflict within Marriage*
 3:00– 3:45 BREAK
 3:45– 4:15 *Session 5: Nonagenda Agenda (Open Group Time)*
 4:15– 5:30 *Session 6: Parenthood*
 5:30– 7:30 DINNER
 7:30– 9:00 *Session 7: Sexuality*
 9:00– 9:30 *Reflections on the Day*

SUNDAY MORNING:
 9:00– 9:30 *Warming Up*
 9:30–10:30 *Session 8: Goal Setting and Financial Planning*
10:30–10:45 BREAK
10:45–11:45 *Session 9: Where Do We Go from Here?*
11:45–12:30 *Evaluation and Closing Worship Celebration*

Though the sample schedule (that is detailed in the next section) contains considerable structure, there is a need to remain open and flexible in designing the weekend and to be aware of participants' needs and interests. Perhaps the group will get into some area that for some reason requires more group time than has been scheduled. If the leadership is inflexible at that point, couples may miss out on exploring an issue critical to their growth.

3. The Arrangements and Setting

It's important that all arrangements for the weekend be completed before the first session begins, with all materials present so that the leadership can give complete attention to developing relationships with the participants.

An informal, comfortable setting is necessary. Room for dividing the group into small clusters (two to six people each) will be needed. A thick rug, a fireplace, easy access to light refreshments and restrooms—all enhance the community-building spirit of the weekend. Retreat centers, old homes that are large, some hotel or motel settings, and comfortable church lounges can all be used. Freedom from the telephone and accessibility of housing accommodations are essential. If the workshop is located near interesting restaurants, couples often enjoy going out to dinner on Saturday night.

Though churches may budget some money for staff leadership in their education budgets, it is good policy to expect participants to share a major portion of the cost for such a weekend. Financial investment often stimulates personal investment.

4. Supplies Needed

Participant materials (see chapter 5)	Magazines
Newsprint and felt-tipped markers	Scissors
16mm Projector and screen	Paste or glue
Pencils or pens	Posterboard
Masking Tape	

5. Use of Participants' Materials

A variety of participants' materials is provided for use in the workshop. It may be helpful to read through those materials (in chapter 5) while reviewing instructions for "conducting the Workshop Sessions" following this section.

In addition to inventories and exercises there is a section called *Description and Log* for each session.

Leaders should use all materials, including the *Description and Log* sections to help achieve the objectives for each session. If the objectives can best be achieved by using the materials mentioned in the next paragraphs, that's fine; but leaders should feel free to modify, drop, or replace materials. In most cases the *Description and Log* is introduced at the beginning of a session. It can be read quickly, either silently by individuals or aloud in the full group. The "Session Overview" provides an occasion to affirm or to modify the agenda; the "Session Outcome" provides additional integrity to the enterprise by letting everyone know what goals are intended to be realized. "Theological Reflections" can be used in a variety of ways: input for couples' discussions together, stimulus for a group discussion, background to the rest of the session, or material for couples to review as part of the follow-up to the weekend.

The *Log* is intended to encourage couples to write their own records, keeping notes in diary form while going through the workshop. At first couples may be hesitant, but as the weekend continues, the logs are likely to become increasingly important. More than any other preprinted material, the participants' own records of feelings and ideas and events will take on deep meaning. It will give couples something to go back to long after the workshop experience itself has passed. Generally, each participant should receive his or her own set of materials and maintain his or her own log; in some cases, however, a leader may elect to provide materials to couples rather than individuals.

The model for Session 9 of this workshop assumes that participants have kept a log throughout the weekend. If couples are not recording their experiences, leaders will need to modify the plan for the final session.

6. Conducting the Workshop Sessions
FRIDAY
SESSION 1: ROLES AND EXPECTATIONS (7:30–10:00, followed by worship).

For background see "Session Overview," "Session Outcome," and "Theological Reflection" in *Description and Log* for Session 1, found in chapter 5.

7:30– 8:15 *Getting Acquainted and Building the Group*

1. *Interview in pairs* (15 minutes). Each person finds someone in the group whom he or she would like to get to know. Take seven minutes to interview this person, using the *Get Acquainted Interview Form* (in chapter 5).

2. *In fours* (10 minutes). Move into groups of four each and introduce your new acquaintance, sharing what you discovered about him or her by means of questions 4 and 6 of the *Get Acquainted Interview Form*. Allow some time for group response.

3. *Whole group* (20 minutes). Have each person take one or two minutes to introduce the partner he or she originally interviewed to the whole group, using the remaining questions of the *Get Acquainted Interview Form*.

8:15– 8:30 *Clarifying the Agenda*

Review the proposed agenda with the group, noting those areas where participants show special interests. More agenda time may be planned for those areas where most need is indicated. As the group reviews the entire agenda, participants will be able to determine where their particular concerns will be treated, and they will see the comprehensive scope of the workshop. Of course, participants' perceptions of their own needs may change considerably during the course of the workshop.

8:30– 8:45 BREAK

8:45– 9:00 *Introduction of Description and Log*

Distribute the *Description and Log* for Session 1 to all participants. Explain that these materials will be kept by participants after the workshop. Review the format, and explain the intended use of each section. Encourage participants to make full use of the *Log*—writing observations, reactions, feelings, ideas, concerns, hopes—in other words, keeping a diary of the weekend.

9:00–10:00 *Role Expectation Inventory*

Have participants complete the *Role Expectation Inventory* (in chapter 5), identifying parental roles and expected roles in their relationships with their partners (fifteen minutes). Then give each couple ten minutes to compare their results with each other, identifying areas of agreement and disagreement. Spend the remainder of the hour allowing couples to explore with the group some of these role expectation differences. Facilitators will need to be sensitive as to how these differences are handled by the couple—both in their communication style and in their parental (including in-law) relationship roles.

For example, leaders should hear couples identifying real issues such as the following: "Sally and I found that in both our homes our mothers usually determined what social contacts we'd have with in-laws and other relatives. We feel a need to share that responsibility equally in our home." Or "Joel and I discovered our parents had different patterns of deciding how money should be spent. We're having some problems sorting out our own pattern."

Before concluding this session, have couples spend a few minutes making notes in their logs.

10:00–10:15 *Closing: Tuning in—Worship*

1. Go around the group and give each person an opportunity to complete the following sentence: "Tonight I learned or relearned that . . . and I feel . . ." Facilitators and lead couples should model this exercise as well as every other one.

2. Move into a circle with the group standing, partners side by side. Have them join their hands. Quietly name each couple, lifting them up to God, celebrating their uniqueness, and asking Him for help in those areas where concerns have already been expressed tonight.

SATURDAY

Session 2: Communication (9:00–10:30)

For background see "Session Overview," "Session Outcome," and "Theological Reflection" in *Description and Log* for Session 2, found in chapter 5.

1. Distribute *Description and Log* for Session 2, and review the material in it.

2. Becoming Aware of Your Feelings (15 minutes, Directions to Group)

   As this session begins, move through the following awareness exercise:

   a. "Close your eyes and center in on your present feelings. Are you tense, relaxed, anxious, expectant? Be aware of the way your body feels. Are your muscles tense? Do you hurt somewhere? How is your stomach doing?" Spend two minutes in silent self-awareness.

   b. (8 minutes) "Let's move around the circle two or three times and identify in a word or a phrase what you are feeling. Feelings are not good or bad in themselves. They simply *are*. They affect us in positive and in negative ways, but you are not necessarily a 'bad' person if you feel angry or a 'good' person if you feel exhilarated. One of the greatest problems in communication between couples is that one partner tends to place a value judgment ('good' or 'bad') on his or her partner's expression of feelings, rather than *acknowledging* these feelings for what they are." Ask participants to identify their present feelings in a word or a phrase.

   c. (5 minutes) "Let's practice acknowledging each other's feelings this morning, using a simple response: 'George, I sense you're really uptight and tense this morning, and that's all right.' Or 'Sally, you talked about feeling really expectant and hopeful, and that's all right.' You may feel a bit awkward at first, not wanting to sound like you are using a formula, but after you learn the pattern, you can develop your own variations." At the close of this exercise the group facilitator may make explicit the importance of tuning in to each other's feelings as the first step in good communication.

3. DESCRIBING YOUR FEELINGS, Part 1[1] (20 minutes)
Many women and most men have difficulty in communication at the point of accurately describing their feelings to their partners. This exercise and the exercises in the second part, which follows, help participants accurately describe their own feelings and understand the feelings of their partners.

   a. Distribute copies of *Ways of Describing Your Feelings* (in chapter 5).
   b. Move into groups of two couples each, all couples remaining in the same general area for later discussion.
   c. Spend a few minutes completing the following exercise for describing one's feelings, and then compare notes with each other in your group of four.
   d. The *Ways of Describing Your Feelings* exercise provides the groups enough examples to illustrate the point that people often express their feelings in a disguised or ambiguous way. A feeling is often hidden behind positive or negative value judgments. Couples can usually get much further in understanding each other if they can develop clear patterns of identifying and expressing their feelings. To make sure learning has actually occurred in the small groups, ask for some feedback to the whole group.

4. EXPLORING OUR FEELINGS, Part 2 (20 minutes)
   a. Remain in the same clusters of four, with each couple taking turns being first the *focus* persons and then the *observers.*

---

[1]This section is modeled after several chapters in David Johnson, *Reaching Out: Interpersonal Effectiveness and Self-Actualization* (Englewood Cliffs, N.J.: Prentice-Hall, 1972), pp. 61-101. Used by permission.

b. (2 minutes) One couple begins by identifying an aspect of their relationship where they sense that more understanding is needed. (It should be an aspect which the couple has agreed to discuss.) Ask the couple to define the situation briefly so that each one in the group has some of the particulars clearly in mind.

c. (6 minutes). Have one partner of each focus couple describe to his or her partner as clearly as possible *both* the feeling generated ("I feel . . ."—a negative feeling) *and* the behavior stimulating the feeling. Example: "I feel overwhelmed when you start talking about all the things we've got to do yet before the wedding."

The other partner responds in an understanding way. For example: "I didn't know you felt so swamped. Is there anything we can do to take some of the pressure off?"

The couples' roles are then reversed, and they repeat the same process.

d. (2 minutes) Observers check out with the couple whether or not they feel closer in their understanding about the issue than before the exercise, and if not, why not.

e. (10 minutes) The entire process is repeated with the couples reversing the focus and observer roles.

f. If time permits, have couples experiment with the description of positive feelings in the same way. For example: One partner says, "When you call me to let me know you'll be late, I really feel appreciated"; then the other partner responds, "It makes me feel pleased to know you appreciate those kinds of little things I do."

5. Total Group Feedback (35 minutes)

a. Move back into the larger group and spend the remaining time sharing the impact of clear communication of feelings. One or two couples may now wish to explore more deeply with each other in the presence of the whole group where their interaction is leading them.

The group leader(s) should help participants distinguish between the kinds of communication (casual, personal, and intimate) and should soon find other couples beginning to *buy into* the full group process.

b. Provide some time for couples to record ideas or impressions in their logs *before* the break occurs.

Note: The exercises described above may seem too obvious to some, but it has been the experience of the author that people often miss the obvious truths and are not able to demonstrate even the most basic, effective communication skills. This process will be a building block for the remainder of the workshop. Time will be given in other sessions to focus on other elements of communication such as the accurate understanding of what we *mean* by what we *say.* But don't assume that most couples who come to the workshop will know basic, effective communication skills; this session is important.

10:30–10:45 BREAK

SESSION 3: SPIRITUALITY (10:45–12:00)
For background see "Session Overview," "Session Outcome," and "Theological Reflection" in *Description and Log* for Session 3, chapter 5.

1. Distribute *Description and Log* for Session 3, and review the material in it.

2. WRITING YOUR OWN COVENANT (30 minutes)
   a. Introduce this session with a statement of the importance of a couple's forming their own definition of their relationship, often publicly summarized in the wedding ceremony. Some couples may wish to work with their minister in shaping a wedding celebration reflecting their own faith as well as the faith of the larger covenant community. The "Theological Reflection" in the *Description and Log* can be used at this point both to

initiate and to shape conversations between and among couples.

b. Give each participant a copy of *Writing Your Own Covenant* (in chapter 5). The sample vows represent a broad range of styles and attitudes toward the marriage relationship. Some vows are articulated in very specific religious language. Others contain little language which is religious in the traditional sense. The intent here is to help couples identify a language of commitment which is appropriate to them.

Ask participants to begin to sketch a brief outline of their own commitment in a language which makes sense to them. Then each couple should be encouraged to spend ten minutes sharing and clarifying with each other the meaning of their initial statements.

3. DISCOVERING STRATEGIES FOR KEEPING OUR COVENANT (45 minutes)

a. Move back into the larger group and encourage couples to react to this experience of writing out their own covenants, especially around points of dissatisfaction and of satisfaction with commitment statements. Limited group time will probably be spent working with one or two couples who especially ask for group help.

b. Lead the group into a time when specific couples identify what spiritual disciplines or strategies might help them keep their commitments to each other and to God.

Examples: A weekly time of talking through rough edges and personal or relationship goals.

A time of prayer following this weekly checking-out period, which would include thanksgiving, confession, and prayer for help.

Reading and discussing literature that focuses on marriage enrichment.

> Periodic experiences of marriage enrichment retreats.
>
> Individual time set aside for personal renewal.
>
> Finding a supportive religious community that meets both partners' needs.

Put these strategies on newsprint or a board as a reminder to the group for the rest of the weekend. Give participants a few minutes of quiet time to write information into their logs, including (if they wish) strategies that were suggested during this session.

Suggest that couples spend time tonight completing their covenant statements in preparation for the closing celebration of worship tomorrow.

12:00–1:00 LUNCH (Encourage participants to get some exercise after lunch.)

SESSION 4: CONFLICT WITHIN MARRIAGE (1:00–3:00)
For background see "Session Overview," "Session Outcome," and "Theological Reflection" in *Description and Log* for Session 4, found in chapter 5.

1. Distribute *Description and Log* for Session 4, and review the material in it.

2. RELAXATION EXERCISES (10 minutes)
   Exercises will allow people to work off excess energy, but even more importantly, they help reduce tension in a tension-building session.

   Suggestions:[2] Neck-shoulder rub.

   > Have one person bend over with arms completely relaxed and hanging. Two other persons give firm karate chops from head to heels and back again; follow with a firm tapping with the ends of the

---

[2]For further suggestions see Bernard Gunther's *Sense Relaxation Below Your Mind* (New York: Collier, 1968), pp. 62-79, or Howard R. Lewis and Harold S. Streitfeld, *Growth Games* (New York: Bantam, 1972), pp. 85-115.

fingers; and conclude with a warm, caring massage of the neck and back.

Take a fantasy trip with relaxing mood music, participants listening to that music while lying on the floor.

3. FILM (or other media) (15 minutes)
   At this point a change to another form of medium is important as stimulus material to help participants recognize feelings of conflict in their own relationships. You may have your own media suggestions. The main point is to be sure you have previewed your material and are convinced it is appropriate for your group.

   Film suggestions: *The Weekend* (15 minutes) or *Handling Marital Conflict* (14 minutes) or *Three Styles of Marital Conflict)* (14 minutes). See other suggestions under "Films" in the Bibliography.

4. GROUP INTERACTION
   a. Spend a few minutes working through some general reactions to the film. Some questions you can ask the group are these: "With what part did you most identify?" "What new learning or strategies did you discover for conflict resolution?"

      If *Handling Marital Conflict* is used, there are two obvious questions to be asked: "Does the suggested pattern of handling conflict work for the two of you? Would anyone like to try it out here in the group?"
   b. Enough structure has already been given to this session. The couples should be able to identify an issue of conflict in their relationship and begin to work with each other within the entire group in fairly open ways. The group becomes a third party. There may be some resistance at this stage on the part of couples to sharing their problems with the whole group. On the other hand, this process has at least begun in earlier sessions.

      If the leader believes more structure is needed

than a film followed by discussion and group work, the following pattern is recommended:

(1) (10 minutes) Have each couple move to a certain place alone and identify an area of conflict or a problem that brings real tension to their relationship. They are to select an issue that both partners want to resolve and to which both partners believe there is some possible solution.

(2) Then have the couples move back into the larger group and ask for a couple to volunteer to work through the various stages of constructive resolution of conflict, using *A Model for the Constructive Handling of Conflict* in chapter 5.

(3) Continue this process with other couples as time permits.

c. Whatever strategy for leading this session is selected, be sure to provide participants sufficient time near the end of the session to record their impressions. This is particularly important because during Session 9 there is a focus on items in participants' logs.

Note: A closing word about the biblical distinction between anger and sin may be helpful. All of us get angry. That's part of our humanity. It is what many do with their anger (hating, hurting others, holding resentments) that makes anger so destructive. Ephesians 4:25ff. ought not be disregarded.

3:00–3:15 BREAK

SESSION 5: NONAGENDA AGENDA (Open Group Time) (3:15–4:15)

For background see "Session Overview," "Session Outcome," and "Theological Reflection" in *Description and Log* for Session 5, found in chapter 5.

1. Distribute *Description and Log* for Session 5, and review the material in it.

2. Encourage couples to spend this time using the group as a sounding board for some aspect of their relationships that they wish to talk about either at greater depth than yet possible or because it is not on the stated agenda.

3. Set aside at least 15 minutes in this session for couples to log their feelings. Depending on group reactions, there may be some helpful reconsideration of the agenda near the close of this session.

SESSION 6: PARENTHOOD (4:15–5:30)
For background see "Session Overview," "Session Outcome," and "Theological Reflection" in *Description and Log* for Session 6, in chapter 5.

1. Distribute *Description and Log* for Session 6, and review the material in it.

2. GETTING IN TOUCH WITH OUR FEELINGS (15 minutes)
Ask each participant to build a collage (on a piece of posterboard) by which each tries to symbolize his or her response to the following questions:

a. How do I feel when I think about becoming a parent?

b. What were some of my best memories about my parents and me?

A variety of materials, including appropriate magazines, must be provided at this point for the building of collages. And while the collage making is being completed, put on the walls a number of key words and phrases related to parenthood. These words and phrases will serve as background for part 4 of this session. Suggested words and phrases to be put on the walls include:

> What about no children?
> How many?
> Family planning?
> Contraceptives—her responsibility?
> Child care
> Discipline
> Strict parents

> Permissive parents
> Dad and the baby
> Baptism—Christian education
> Are you ready?
> What about my career?
> Everything changes when baby comes!
> No more time alone?

3. SHARING OUR REFLECTIONS (20 minutes)
   Move into the larger group and suggest that each person briefly share some part of his or her collage and its meaning.

4. IDENTIFYING KEY ISSUES (40 minutes)
   Invite couples to identify their most important current question with regard to parental concerns. The goal is not to give "air time" to every couple in this area. Rather, work with a few couples to show *feeling* and *content* levels about which partners must communicate with as much understanding and advance information as possible. The lead couple may be good resource people for information, but it is even more important that couples begin to communicate honestly their feelings and expectations about becoming parents. It is especially important for those who have real doubts about wanting to become parents to express these feelings in the safety of the group. It's seldom true that partners have really explored this area while they are engaged. Their differences with each other may be surprising.

5. Encourage participants to take a few minutes to record feelings—both positive and negative—about parenthood. They might want to work quietly a few minutes, answering the question, "What feelings do I have when I look ahead and see myself as a parent? as a nonparent?"

5:30–7:30 DINNER

By this point in the weekend couples are usually ready to get away for a while and have a leisurely meal. A list of recommended restaurants in the immediate area will help participants who aren't familiar with the area. If a meal is planned at a retreat center, it's worth the extra cost and effort to make it especially pleasant by providing mood music and by providing time for partners to be alone for a while.

SESSION 7: SEXUALITY (7:30–9:00)
For background see "Session Overview," "Session Outcome," and "Theological Reflection" in *Description and Log* for Session 7, in chapter 5.

1. Distribute *Description and Log* for Session 7 and review the material in it.

2. INTRODUCTION (5-10 minutes)
Introduce this session by pointing out that tonight's theme focuses on communication around sexuality, not on the physiology of sex and sex technique. Encourage couples to spend time with one's partner, working through some resource material on the physical, emotional, and spiritual aspects of sexual relating. (Such follow-up material is listed in the Bibliography of this manual.)

A sample of the cassette tapes of Dr. Ed Wheat—a series entitled *Sex Problems and Sex Techniques in Marriage*—might be played as an illustration of the kind of follow-up resources that are available. A congregation or a cluster of churches might consider obtaining a library section of several kinds of follow-up resources.

In addition the use of the humorous film clip *Love Toads* or other brief audiovisuals may help to relieve some of the anxiety surrounding the discussion theme.

3. GROWING UP SEXUAL (25 minutes)
Participants can profit from an exchange of past experiences concerning sexual knowledge and awareness. Couples will be able to use this background information for understanding each other's attitudes towards sex and sexual relating. A person's experience during the growing-up

years affects both one's ability to enjoy one's own sexuality
and to give pleasure to one's partner.

Arrange the group in two concentric circles, women
on the inside facing out and men on the outside facing in.
Invite each group member to share with the partner opposite him or her a response to question one below, each
taking ninety seconds for his or her answer; women answer
first, followed by the men. At the end of a three-minute
segment have the men shift to the left for another question
and mutual response. Move around the circle, with the
men shifting each time until all the questions have been
discussed.

Questions: 1. As a child how did you understand or sense
your parents' physical-sexual relationship with
each other?
2. What was the place of touching one another and
the open display of affection in the total family?
3. What were some of your earliest feelings about
being a boy or a girl?
4. What kinds of feelings did you have about nud-
ity and about your body?
5. What are your first memories of sexual awareness, such as playing doctor?
6. How did your parents handle sex education?
What did they teach you about the right way to
behave with the opposite sex?
7. What were your first ideas about sexual intercourse?
8. What did you feel was God's attitude toward
your sexual feelings and struggles?

4. GROUP EXPLORATION (60 minutes)
Help the group make the transition from their past experiences to the issues most important to their present relationships. The following excerpt from an interview with a
couple eighteen months after marriage may help focus the
group discussion:

WIFE: Another area we would suggest engaged couples work on is sex. I don't mean only intercourse but also such areas as simply being affectionate.

HUSBAND: Yeah, when we were dating, this was never a problem, but I find that I need much less affection than Jan, so sometimes I have to be affectionate whether I feel like it or not, because she needs it.

WIFE: Yes, I like to curl up together with him watching TV, or just having him hug me now and then. I need that.

INTERVIEWER: The next question is rather personal; don't feel obligated to answer it. But do you feel you were adequately prepared sexually for marriage?

HUSBAND: We didn't go all the way before marriage, but it wasn't all that good the first week—in fact, it was a little disappointing.

WIFE: Sometimes I almost wish we hadn't waited, yet I'm glad we did. But it was hard because I felt so guilty even getting close that, after we were married, it was hard to get used to that idea.

INTERVIEWER: Do you think it would have helped if the minister would have spoken about this beforehand?

WIFE: Our minister? He'd never say anything.

HUSBAND: No, I don't think he would have even dared speak of it.

WIFE: But I think it would have been good.

Use this excerpt as a role play with some suggested questions for the group like the following:

(1) What effect does your own growing-up experience of sexuality have on your sexual relating to your partner?
(2) Were there particular points in the role play with which you as a couple identified?
(3) What concerns not yet expressed are you as a couple working through?
(4) It is often said that men and women approach sexual relating quite differently. How do you react to this statement from your experience as a couple?

Again, it will be important for the facilitator(s) to help couples center on their own patterns of communication with each other about sexual concerns rather than on a discussion about sex that is emotionally distant from their actual experience. Here is a place where the lead couple may really be helpful with some modeling of their own communication style.

Note: The exercise and questions used in section 3, GROW-ING UP SEXUAL, were suggested by a viewer's guide produced by Iowa State University (1976) to accompany a television series entitled "Living Married."

9:00–9:30 *Reflections on the Day*

This last half-hour can be a good time for helping couples *begin* to summarize what the day has meant for them and discover where they have made some progress with each other. This need not be a lengthy period, particularly since everyone will be ready for a break. But it's almost always an affectionate (mellow) time, without an abrupt transition from the session on sexuality to the wrapping-up process. Individuals may wish to reach out in affirmation or appreciation to someone else in the group.

Remind couples to bring with them their beginning statements of commitment to each other tomorrow, which they started this morning.

Encourage participants to spend a few minutes later recording final reactions to all the events of this day in their logs.

SUNDAY

9:00–9:30 *Warming Up*

Begin the day with some nonverbal exercises, which may help couples sense the importance of both verbal and nonverbal elements in communication.[3]

---

[3]Other suggestions may be found in Johnson, *Reaching Out*, pp. 103-14, and in Howard Clinebell, Jr., *The People Dynamic: Changing Self and Society Through Growth Groups* (New York: Harper and Row, 1972), p. 46-52.

Suggestions:

1. (10 minutes) Sit opposite your partner, and close your eyes. Explore through touch each other's hands and face and torso. Be gentle, and communicate caring and tenderness. After about five minutes open your eyes and talk with each other about how you felt while giving and receiving.

2. (10 minutes) Imagine that your partner is going away for a very lengthy trip. Express your feelings toward your partner without using words. Then express your feelings in words. How do you compare and contrast the two avenues of communication? Discuss this experience in the whole group.

3. (10 minutes) Imagine you have some negative feelings (fear, anger, pain, resentment) about something. Express your feelings nonverbally. Then use words to communicate how you feel along with the nonverbal expression. Discuss with each other this question: "How would it be helpful for me to change the way I express my negative feelings?"

   Note: Often one partner is confused about nonverbal expressions of feeling, not knowing at what or to whom or about what the feeling is really directed. Partners should be made aware of this fact. For example, the following statement is typical: "When my partner is angry with herself, I often feel that she is angry with me until we talk it through. All I sense is her nonverbal, facial expression of irritation or pain and her physical withdrawal from me."

Session 8: Goal Setting and Financial Planning (9:30–10:30)

For background see "Session Overview," "Session Outcome," and "Theological Reflection" in *Description and Log* for Session 8, chapter 5.

1. Distribute *Description and Log* for Session 8 and review the material in it. Explain to participants that the approach

in this session is one of strengthening communication patterns about careers and financial planning. If couples would like more specific information or assistance, suggestions are available in "For Follow-up," chapter 6, in this manual.

2. WHAT ARE THE PATTERNS? (5 minutes)
Ask participants to take the *Role Expectation Inventory* which was used Friday night, and review their responses to questions that dealt specifically with career and finances—for example: responses 1, 2, and 3 (outside the home) and responses 1 and 7 (inside the home). Questions 38-41 of the *Marriage Expectation Inventory* also touch briefly on these issues.

3. WHAT ARE THE KEY ISSUES? (10 minutes)
Ask each couple to summarize together in brief outline form a basic career and money management pattern for the next five years. This is to include such items as working plans, selecting a place to live (renting or buying), major purchases necessary or desired, any children planned and related expenses, travel, insurance, etc. Have the couples jot down (in their logs) any fears, barriers, or tensions which they discover—or are already aware of—surrounding these issues.

4. EXPLORING THESE ISSUES (45 minutes)
Spend group time working with individual couples around decision-making concerns and areas of conflict needing further negotiation. Couples may discover that they agree about their basic attitudes and role expectations or that they still have some very real differences that did not get handled in the group either on Friday night or that have surfaced since that time.

Give participants at least three or four minutes while they are still in the group setting to make notes in their logs concerning the areas of goal setting and financial planning.

10:30–10:45 BREAK

SESSION 9: WHERE DO WE GO FROM HERE?

For background see "Session Overview," "Session Outcome,"
and "Theological Reflection" in *Description and Log* for Session 9, chapter 5.

1. IDENTIFYING PERSONAL GROWTH AND LEARNING (10 minutes)
   Present, in role play form, two other excerpts from the
   couple's interview that was introduced last night.

Excerpt 1:

INTERVIEWER: What kind of suggestions would you give me for
               helping a couple establish a good relationship?

WIFE: I would say the first thing would be to do a lot of
               things together. Just spend time together. When
               Tom and I were at Indiana State University, we
               both had to stay there during Thanksgiving
               vacation—and we spent time with each other
               every day—a lot of time—whenever we weren't
               working. That really helped our relationship. I
               guess another thing would be that they have hon-
               est communication. We took a class together at
               ISU in interpersonal relationships. That forced us
               to communicate and helped us work through a lot
               of problems before marriage.

HUSBAND: Yeah, and it's important to be able to open up—
               and trust the other person. Another area would be
               to know yourself so that you can communicate.

INTERVIEWER: Do you think age makes any difference here?

HUSBAND: No, not really. We weren't very old when we got
               married, so that really depends on the person, not
               age.

INTERVIEWER: Well, are there other areas?

WIFE: Yes, well—maybe this doesn't belong here, but we
               had to learn not to cut each other with jokes. You
               know, those jokes which are more than fun—but
               were meant or said from a hurting point of view.

INTERVIEWER: Hey, these things will be helpful. Another ques-
               tion that is similar to the first is, What areas would

be good for me to explore with a couple in premarital counseling?

HUSBAND: Well, like we said—look to see whether they have similar interests, if they do things together they both enjoy. This also may include whether they have similar values. Also, I'd want them to be prepared for rough times.

WIFE: Finances would be a good thing to go over. We've got a lot more expense—with the house, insurance, etc., than we had before marriage, and how you're going to spend the little you have left can be a real hassle.

Excerpt 2:

HUSBAND: One other thing you might look at is how they express anger—or whether they do express anger. We express or show it in different ways, and I think it's because our families show it in different ways.

WIFE: Yes, Dave will show his anger, you know, by yelling it out. But I just get quiet, and I really had a hard time with that at first. I really thought he hated me, but as we both learned more of each other, we saw that it's just different ways of expressing anger.

HUSBAND: Yes, my family is one that lets it all hang out. But hers doesn't, so we had to learn to adjust here.

INTERVIEWER: Another question that I feel we've touched on but needs to be spun out a little is, "How easy or hard was it to move from a single life to a married life?"

WIFE: Well, one thing is that you have to be prepared for work—there's all that housework and cleaning and the laundry—now that's the worst of all, and buying groceries. And another area (hesitation here) at least I had trouble with was sleeping with another person. I wasn't really used to it. Dave helps in all these things because we both work, but it's a lot more work than I realized.

HUSBAND: Another thing is that your mate becomes your best friend. You don't run around with the guys or girls like you used to—but I really never did much of that anyway. You also have more money when you're single, but not a whole lot more because we were both students. Another thing is that you have to get used to living with the fact that the other person will always be there even when you don't feel like having him or her around. When you were single, you could just go back to your room, but now you have to learn to communicate even during those times when you'd rather be alone.

2. Distribute *Description and Log* for Session 9, and review the material in it. Make sure participants have all their logs available from previous sessions.

3. INDIVIDUAL COUPLES (20 minutes)
   a. Ask couples to go back through all the logs they've made and together select at least two areas in their relationship that they both consider to be strong—and one area that they both agree needs some specific further work.
   b. Then have the couples identify some strategies for strengthening their relationship, using insights and skills learned (or rediscovered) during this workshop.

4. GROUP SUPPORT (30 minutes)
   Invite each couple to share briefly some of their learnings and follow-up strategies. Encourage the group to identify for each couple some strengths which have been observed during the weekend that may help them follow through with constructive change. As this is carefully done, the group will begin to sense a real spirit of caring and appreciation for having been with each other.

11:45–12:30 *Evaluation and Closing Worship Celebration*

1. Have each person complete a brief written evaluation, perhaps using the *Evaluation Form* found in chapter 5 or one similar to it.

2. Distribute a list of follow-up suggestions (see "For Follow-up," chapter 6).

3. Close with an appropriate time of worship, using the covenant statements couples have written.
4. Suggested Model of Worship:
   a. A song of celebration.
   b. Prayers of confession where covenants have already been broken.
   c. Some scriptural words of assurance.
   d. A scripture lesson (see texts cited in "Theological Reflection").
   e. Prayers of thanksgiving.
      [Form a circle, and ask one couple at a time to stand in the center. Encourage the group to make that couple the focus of their prayers, both silently and audibly in sentence prayers. The group may even want to lay their hands on the couple.]
   f. A charge and a benediction.

Final Note: In some weekend workshops couples will recognize during the course of the weekend that they have serious doubts about continuing their engagement and planning their marriage. If those doubts are substantial or well-founded, the weekend has served a valuable, if unhappy, function.

It is particularly important that when such happens, that such couples receive the support of the group, the continuing prayers of all who have shared this time with these couples, and the ongoing counsel of their pastor(s) and the workshop leader(s).

CHAPTER
5

Participants'
Materials

THE MARRIAGE EXPECTATION INVENTORY
FORM I: FOR ENGAGED COUPLES

Directions

The procedure for taking the inventory is simple:
Set aside two hours and separate yourself from your future spouse so you cannot see what he or she is writing.
Thoughtfully fill in your form as honestly as possible.
When ready, come back together to share your answers.

Part I: Love in Marriage

1. Love is usually having to say:

---

2. Since we first met, the following changes have taken place in our relationship:

3. Describe several instances when your future partner demonstrated real love toward you during the last month.

4. Describe several situations in which you, intentionally or unintentionally were hurtful to your future partner in the last month.

5. Give the ways you and your future husband (wife) differ.

6. Give the ways you and your future husband (wife) are alike.

7. Describe some specific things your future partner has "bugged" you about recently which you could have corrected but didn't:

8. What are the strengths you will bring to your marriage?

9. What are the strengths your future partner will bring to your marriage?

10. How will you use your strong points to grow together in love after marriage?

11. What are some of the weaknesses you will bring to your marriage?

12. What are some of your future partner's weaknesses?

13. In our marriage, love will grow primarily by:

14. When you (write a positive comment about your future partner):

    I feel (write a positive emotion that you feel):

15. When you (write a negative comment about your future partner):

    I feel (write a negative emotion about yourself):

Part II: Communication in Marriage

16. Communication means to me:

17. I feel most like communicating with my future partner when:

18. I feel least like communicating with my future partner when:

19. Describe several things which your future partner does which make it easy to share yourself with him (her).

20. Describe several things your future partner does which make it difficult to share yourself with him (her).

21. Describe how you plan to make important decisions in your marriage.

22. In our marriage, communication will be so important that:

23. As far as communication in our future marriage, one partner:

24. One aspect(s) of our relationship I've been reluctant to discuss with my future partner, but wish to now, is:

Part III: Freedom in Marriage

25. My idea of freedom in marriage is:

26. Freedom to:

    implies a corresponding obligation to:

27. Describe several ways you've learned to balance personal freedom with responsibility to your future partner.

28. The most difficult area for me to allow my future partner freedom in is:

29. Some areas where I feel a lack of freedom with my future partner are:

Part IV: Sex in Marriage

30. Describe some ways love and sex are related.

31. Describe several ways that sex has become of greater or lesser importance in your relationship.

32. When it comes to sexual pleasure my needs:

and my future partner's needs:

33. Sexual experience without love is:

and love without sex is:

34. I feel most comfortable with my future husband (wife) when:

35. I feel most uncomfortable with my future husband (wife) when:

36. My feelings about family planning are:

37. Decisions about family planning should be made by:

    taking into consideration:

Part V: Money

38. Money in our future family will mean:

39. Describe how financial decisions will be made in your future family.

40. Major sources of conflict in our money matters are related to:

41. I feel:

about a working wife.

Explain:

Part VI: Selfishness

42. Selfishness to me:

43. Selfishness in my relationship has been:

Part VII: Religious Expectations

44. Religious belief and practice in our marriage will mean:

45. Describe several religious attitudes you like about your future partner.

46. Describe several religious attitudes you dislike about your future partner.

47. I feel religion in the home:

48. Responsibility for the religious education of our children:

Part VII: Relatives
49. Describe several things about your future partner's parents that you really like.

50. Describe several things about your future partner's parents that you dislike.

51. As far as I'm concerned, my parents:

52. As far as I'm concerned, my future partner's parents:

53. My future in-laws need to learn right now:

as far as our marriage is concerned.

Part IX: Expectations Related to Children

54. How many children would be the ideal number in our family?

55. For me the ideal child:

56. Describe some of the ways to best help your children grow and mature.

57. List the changes you plan to make from your parents' child rearing practices.

58. In a happy family, children should be:

and not:

GET ACQUAINTED FORM

INTRODUCTIONS—(Interview in pairs)

1. Name:

2. Partner's name:

3. How long have you known each other? How did you meet?

4. What are you most proud of?
   a. Individually

   b. As a couple

5. List three sections of the *Marriage Expectation Inventory* that you would like to discuss this weekend:
   a.

b.

c.

6. What do you see yourself doing or being five years from now?

Description and Log: Session 1

ROLES AND EXPECTATIONS

Couples will review the role patterns established in their parents' homes and based on that review will identify their own expected role patterns for marriage.

Couples should be able to identify and resolve significant differences in role expectations.

Couples should be able to anticipate changes in relationships to their parents.

"Be subject to one another out of reverence for Christ" (Ephesians 5:21).

Like corporations with one boss at the top some families can only operate with one person in charge. Typically it's been the husband and father. Sometimes domineering, rarely cruel, usually generous—the masculine authority has traditionally ruled the roost.

Sometimes, however, the strong partner has been the wife and mother. When this becomes a sociological pattern, sociologists notice; we hear all about matriarchal family structures. And when this becomes gossip, everyone notices and whispers: "Guess who wears the pants in *that* family?"

The Christian couple headed for marriage should look beyond mere tradition or sociological patterns. There's a much better model in the New Testament, and the key principle in this model is, "Be subject to one another. . . ." We learn this principle from Christ, who taught us less about giving orders than about obeying them. While others spoke of His kingship, He moved among us like a servant (Phil. 2:1-8). He filled a role no one had expected Him to.

But what are your expectations in this regard, and what roles do you project for your marriage? That's the focus of this session. And while you're working on those questions, you might recall two others: What roles does God intend for Christians to fill in their marriages? What are His expectations for Christians in their marriages?

PERSONAL
LOG:

ROLE EXPECTATION INVENTORY

As you complete the inventory, fill in both the left and the right columns, indicating the role pattern in your parents' home in the left column and the anticipated role pattern in your own home in the right column.[1]

Roles or Functions Outside the Home

Primarily Husband	Primarily Wife	Both Share		Primarily Husband	Primarily Wife	Both Share
☐	☐	☐	1. Decides husband's place of work.	☐	☐	☐
☐	☐	☐	2. Decides whether wife works.	☐	☐	☐
☐	☐	☐	3. Decides where and when wife works.	☐	☐	☐
☐	☐	☐	4. Coordinates children's school and community functions.	☐	☐	☐
☐	☐	☐	5. Volunteers in other community functions (e.g., fire company, local government).	☐	☐	☐
☐	☐	☐	6. Decides on local church and level of involvement.	☐	☐	☐
☐	☐	☐	7. Coordinates social involvement.	☐	☐	☐
☐	☐	☐	8. Determines number of and scheduling of personal interests.	☐	☐	☐
☐	☐	☐	9. Coordinates social involvement with in-laws and relatives.	☐	☐	☐

[1]Adapted from *Living Married*, Cooperative Extension Services, Iowa, Minnesota, North Dakota, South Dakota, and Wisconsin, 1974, Curtiss Hall, Iowa State University, Ames, Iowa.

Roles or Functions Inside the Home

Parents' Home   ### Your Home

Primarily Husband	Primarily Wife	Both Share		Primarily Husband	Primarily Wife	Both Share
☐	☐	☐	1. Determines where the family will live.	☐	☐	☐
☐	☐	☐	2. Decides whether you have children and how many.	☐	☐	☐
☐	☐	☐	3. Teaches values to children and manages discipline.	☐	☐	☐
☐	☐	☐	4. Handles household shopping.	☐	☐	☐
☐	☐	☐	5. Handles household cleaning.	☐	☐	☐
☐	☐	☐	6. Handles household repairs and maintenance.	☐	☐	☐
☐	☐	☐	7. Handles the finances and keeping of records.	☐	☐	☐
☐	☐	☐	8. Determines amount and use of family time.	☐	☐	☐
☐	☐	☐	9. Gives support to family members.	☐	☐	☐
☐	☐	☐	10. Initiates love and affection toward partner.	☐	☐	☐

DESCRIPTION AND LOG: SESSION 2

COMMUNICATION

SESSION
OVERVIEW: Couples will practice expressing, identifying, and responding to statements that communicate feelings (intimate communication).

SESSION
OUTCOME: Couples should be able to recognize and engage in intimate personal communication.

Couples should value intimate communication.

THEOLOGICAL
REFLECTION: "But the angel said to the women, 'Do not be afraid; for I know that you seek Jesus who was crucified. He is not here; for he has risen . . .'" (Matthew 28:5,6).

Some people think a person is really just a soul. They pray strenuously for souls to be saved on mission fields but don't care enough for bodies still attached to those souls to fight world hunger. On the other hand, a quick peek at B. F. Skinner's psychology or *Playboy*'s centerfold will show that some people believe a person is really just a body.

Similarly, when you listen to some people talk, it seems only emotions are important. They are forever inquiring, "What do you feel about that issue?" When they have time, they go searching, as they say, for their own "true feelings," only to announce that they "feel very deeply about this." Overall, though, the feelers may get outnumbered by the thinkers. Thinkers don't have feelings at all. They only have thoughts.

For all such people—and any others who

want to divide people into parts—there's a powerful, simple lesson in the resurrection of Jesus Christ: wholeness. A person is whole. It wasn't just Jesus' body or just Jesus' soul—it was Jesus. And on resurrection morning it was Jesus stepping out of the tomb. And weekly the Apostles' Creed reminds us of "the resurrection of the body," a confession that people will still be whole even after death.

Between now and our resurrection something of that wholeness should rub off on our communication. Especially in marriage it's important to communicate wholly so that we can know each other wholly—what we think and what we feel, the needs of our bodies and the agony of our souls. Complete communication brings intimacy; anything less than complete communication prevents intimacy.

PERSONAL
LOG:

Ways of Describing Your Feelings

Instructions: Place a check in front of the statement that most clearly describes what the person is feeling.

Example 1:

- ☐ a. Knock it off! I don't want to talk about it.
- ☐ b. When we start talking about that subject, I really get uptight.

Example 2:

- ☐ a. I had a terrible day at work today.
- ☐ b. I really got depressed at work today.
- ☐ c. I felt down most of the day after that departmental meeting.

Example 3:

- ☐ a. You're a wonderful wife, Nancy!
- ☐ b. I really feel supported by you, Nancy!

Example 4:

- ☐ a. Your mother has done it again!
- ☐ b. I don't think I'll ever be able to get along with your mother.
- ☐ c. I really feel rejected by the way your mother centers her attention on you and leaves me out of the conversation when we're all together.

DESCRIPTION AND LOG: SESSION 3

SPIRITUALITY

SESSION
OVERVIEW: Couples will begin development of a covenant statement for their marriage that reflects God's covenant relationship with His people.

SESSION
OUTCOME: Couples should be able to complete and affirm a covenant statement for their marriage.

Couples should value the importance of faithfulness in a marriage (covenant) relationship.

THEOLOGICAL
REFLECTION: "How can I give you up . . . ? (Hosea 11:8).

The act of marriage is a covenant. It involves a set of vows in which two people legally promise to faithfully uphold certain conditions toward one another.

What makes a covenant last is, of course, covenant *keeping*. Another word for that is *faithfulness*.

During the course of this session you'll be discussing spiritual aspects of marriage. But you need to think of more than prayer, Bible reading, or church attendance. You need to think about the whole meaning of the marriage covenant and the whole meaning of covenant faithfulness.

In the Old Testament prophecy of Hosea God is pictured as a faithful husband who is meticulously faithful to the marriage vow. And in the prophecy God's people are seen in the aggregate, as an unfaithful wife, a whore who violates her covenant with giggling abandon. But the marriage was maintained. Instead of acting within the law and stoning his wife, the faithful husband (God) acted with forgiving love and whispered, "How can I give you up . . .?" Covenant (or spiritual) faithfulness, you see, goes far beyond singing hymns—all the way to forgiving unfaithful partners.

At the act of marriage a Christian relationship is sealed in a three-way covenant between God and two of His children. Thereafter, everything that builds or destroys faithfulness is truly a "spiritual" issue.

It's a very demanding covenant. It takes in everything from the bed to the pew. It deserves some discussion together.

PERSONAL
LOG:

WRITING YOUR OWN COVENANT

The following examples of wedding vows reflect a broad spectrum of values and attitudes of couples as they approach their marriage relationship. As you read them, look for those statements with which you most identify and for those statements that challenge your thinking.

1. Mary Jo: A ray of sunshine on a cloudy day,
A breath of spring air after winter's slumber,
A sunflower growing full and radiant.
Understanding and warmth,
Vitality and vigor,
Growth and trust.
These I bring to you, but even greater
is my commitment to our lives as one.

   Gary: I promise to love and respect you,
to share the joys and sorrows together,
to understand each other through periods of
trial and happiness.
I intend to fulfill this promise each new day of
our lives.

2. Steve: I take you, Sandy, as my wife, to love, cherish, and nourish as Christ does the Church, His Body. I will guide you through sickness and health, through good times and bad. I will by God's help lead you as we learn about Him who holds us together with a love stronger than our own. I will always be a faithful and loving husband and father as we build our home. I give you this ring as an outward symbol expressing the everlasting love that is in my heart.

   Sandy: I take you, Steve, as my husband, to love and cherish as the church does Christ, her head. I will always look to you for guidance, through sickness and health, through good times and bad. I will by God's help learn through you about Him who by grace has given us each other. I will always be a trustworthy and faithful wife and mother as we build our home. I give you this ring as an outward symbol of the everlasting love for you that is in my heart.

3.   Sandi: John, I will love and comfort you, share joys and sorrows with you, be your friend and partner, be open with you and listen to you.

                I will respect your rights and allow you to be an individual, give you my approval, and cherish our union.

      John: Sandi, you are a sensitive and loving person, filled with emotion. That emotion has touched me, kindling the spark of love within me, allowing me to see and feel the life which love brings. Come, share that life with me.

Sandi and
      John: I choose you (John, Sandi) for my (husband, wife), to be my friend and companion. I will love and comfort you, I will share the joys and sorrows with you, be open with you and listen to you. I give you this ring; wear it with love.

4.   Peggy: I give you my hand,
I give you my love more precious than money,
I give you myself before preaching and law.
Will you give me yourself? Will you come travel with me?
Shall we stick by each other as long as we live?

   Dennis: Before our families and before my God, I promise to love and respect you and be honest and open with you—when you are happy, when you are sad, when you are sick, and when problems arise that put our love to the

test. I will try to affirm that love each new day
of our lives.

5.   Rick:
       Linda: I (Rick, Linda), take you (Linda, Rick), to be
                 my wedded (wife, husband). With Christ as
                 my example, I give you my life, trusting our
                 love will grow as our love for God grows. I
                 promise to love, understand, forgive, encour-
                 age, and trust you as long as my life here on
                 earth shall last.

Now jot down key words, phrases, or sentences that
come to you as being central in your commitment to your
partner.

DESCRIPTION AND LOG: SESSION 4

CONFLICT WITHIN MARRIAGE

SESSION
OVERVIEW:

Couples will—through physical exercise, discussion of a film, and group interaction—identify destructive and constructive means for handling conflict within marriage.

SESSION:
OUTCOME:

Couples should be able to recognize destructive, and plan constructive, means for handling conflict within marriage.

Couples should anticipate times of conflict within marriage as times for potential growth.

THEOLOGICAL
REFLECTION:

"So if you are offering your gift at the altar, and there remember that your brother has something against you, leave your gift there before the altar and go; first to be reconciled to your brother, and then come and offer your gift." (Matthew 5:23,24).

Marriages come apart. That's not a pleasant reality, of course, but it is a reality. Some marriages that collapse began with two hopeful, committed Christian people in the beginning.

Conflict within marriage isn't very pleasant, either. And all marriages, those that are coming apart and those that are growing stronger, those that are Christian and those that are not—*all* marriages endure conflict. It's not until after the first wave of conflict has washed by that a marriage shows the effects of Christian faith, because although Christians aren't perfect—they should be forgiving.

The lesson Jesus taught in Matthew 5:23,24 has interesting implications for marriage. In Christ's illustration the person leaves the altar not because he has something against someone else but because someone else has something against him. We are called, therefore, not simply to be healed but to be *healers* in our relationships. We not only forgive others; we also seek their forgiveness.

When we forgive each other in marriage, we are doing more than following a moral principle. We are imitating Christ. We know how to forgive because we've been forgiven by Him. In those moments of forgiveness the climate for growth in a marriage is just right.

PERSONAL
LOG:

A MODEL FOR THE CONSTRUCTIVE HANDLING OF CONFLICT

1. The couple faces each other, holds hands, and looks into each other's eyes. One partner volunteers to be the confronter, the other the one being confronted. The group acts as the observor-facilitator and helps the couple progress through each of the stages of the conflict and resolution.
2. The confronting partner completes the following sentence: "One of the things that you do that hurts our relationship is. . . ."

   Try to put this in a way that describes the visible behavior of the other person.

   Example: "Bill, you lose your temper at me too easily when we do not agree right away on a decision."
3. The confronted partner then responds by restating the conflict in his or her own words until both agree on the basic statement of the conflict.
4. The confronting partner then describes his or her feelings or reactions to the other's behavior.

   Example: "Every time you do that, I get irritated with you and am unable to think clearly."
5. The confronted partner also expresses his or her feelings elicited by the conflict.

   Example: "When you get irritated, I just want to avoid you until we both cool down."
6. A process follows in which each partner looks at the way he/she may contribute to the solution of the problem.

   Example: Confronting partner:

   "I can see now how my being on edge really ruins my thinking."

   Confronted partner:

   "I can also see how my fear about getting the short end of the stick gets me ticked off early."

7. This honest, open interaction usually brings negative and
   uncomfortable feelings to a less intense level. The couple
   in our example then look at ways in which they may do the
   following:
   a. Tune into each other's feelings when hard decisions
      arise.
   b. Express acceptance of each partner's freedom to
      suggest alternatives. Avoid making put-downs and
      value judgments.
   c. Agree to seek more information if necessary.
   d. Agree to consider each other's needs in the decision
      making.
   e. Identify personal changes in behavior that would help
      resolve the conflict.
   f. Choose another time to explore the issue if either part-
      ner is not ready to do so when the climate seems un-
      comfortable.

This may appear to be a contrived and complex process,
but every mutual pattern of resolving a conflict takes some
careful and intentional work on the part of both partners.

Adapted from David W. Johnson, *Reaching Out: Interpersonal Effectiveness and Self-Actualization* (Englewood Cliffs, N.J.: Prentice-Hall,
1972), pp. 159-68, 195-201.

DESCRIPTION AND LOG: SESSION 5

NONAGENDA AGENDA

SESSION
OVERVIEW: Within the whole group, couples will discuss
concerns about their relationships and receive
guidance and support from other couples.

SESSION
OUTCOME: Couples should be able to identify and discuss
issues not specifically raised, or not resolved,
in earlier sessions.

THEOLOGICAL
REFLECTION: "Bear one anothers burdens. . . . each one
will have to bear his own load" (Galatians
6:2,5).

When an actress is continually asked to
play only one kind of role, she's apt to lament
her fate and complain that she is hopelessly
typecast. Everyone thinks she can do only one
kind of acting.

Sometimes we typecast in the church,
too. People are leaders or they're followers,
they're gifted or they're inferior, they give or
they take. In fact, it's sometimes very hard for
people in the church to break out of categories
into which we've put them.

But then, think about this workshop.
Which couples have we already typecast as
either talkers or listeners? Are participants
either actively supporting or getting support?

Be careful. Effective relationships—
between husbands and wives, between church
members, between couples in this
workshop—are not built on those kinds of
"either . . . or" roles. Rather, strong relationships must be built on Paul's instructions to

the Galatians. We do not *either* "bear one another's burdens" *or* "each one bear his own load."

There is no "either/or" choice; there's only the "both/and. . . ." Isn't that right?

PERSONAL
   LOG:

Description and Log: Session 6

PARENTHOOD

SESSION
OVERVIEW: Couples will begin to explore some key questions that influence decisions regarding parenthood.

SESSION
OUTCOME: Each person should be able to describe at least one of his or her partner's concerns regarding parenthood.

Couples should be motivated (and provided a model) to make some joint decisions regarding parenthood and to make those decisions before marriage.

THEOLOGICAL
REFLECTION: "Therefore be imitators of God, as beloved children. And walk in love, as Christ loved us and gave himself up for us, a fragrant offering and sacrifice to God" (Ephesians 5:1,2).

Not long ago being an imitator of God with regard to parenthood was really very simple. As God created Adam (the Man) and Eve (the Woman) in His image, married couples were to procreate children in their images. A couple with many children seemed, at least in the eyes of some, more Christian than a childless couple. The first marriage was said to be blessed; the second was judged hollow, fruitless, unfulfilled.

But it has become increasingly evident in recent years that to be imitators of God, to give ourselves up in this area of parenthood, for some may take us in quite another direction. When young couples see swollen bellies of starving children and know that one factor causing starvation is overpopulation, they may recall that God put no more people in the Garden of Eden that could eat well there. In 1 Corinthians 7 Paul urged some to remain single for the sake of the kingdom. Perhaps in our times some will be called to be childless (at least *biologically* childless) for the sake of the kingdom.

Parenthood (pro or con) ought not to be decided on selfish grounds of convenience, personal freedom, or financial assets. But the option to remain childless for the sake of the kingdom—that's something else again.

To be "imitators of God, as beloved children," we must be responsible stewards of His world. And as responsible stewards, the call to "walk in love, as Christ loved us and gave himself up for us," may be a call to give up the joys of parenthood for the cause of Him who loved us.

PERSONAL
LOG:

DESCRIPTION AND LOG: SESSION 7

SEXUALITY

SESSION
OVERVIEW:

Couples will review attitudes and ideas that shaped their current perspective on sexuality and will identify concerns and hopes for sexual fulfillment in their marriage relationship.

SESSION
OUTCOME:

Couples should be able to discuss ideas and feelings about sexuality without anxiety.

Couples should value the importance of sexuality to marriage.

THEOLOGICAL
REFLECTION:

"Then the eyes of both were opened, and they knew that they were naked . . ." (Genesis 3:7).

"Therefore, if any one is in Christ, he is a new creation; the old has passed away, behold, the new has come" (2 Corinthians 5:17).

In biblical perspective the troubles of sexuality all began in the garden, God's garden. There He placed a gardener, our first parent, to do the gardening. Then God gave him a wife. As time went on, our parents wanted to stop gardening and "have a go" at owning. In history's most regretable choice they reached too far and fell. Because God had created the man to be His gardener, in gardening he was now cursed (Gen. 3:17-19). Because one person was lonely, God had made two; and now the means of their most intimate union, sexuality, suffered in the tragedy of human failure (Gen. 3:16).

But Eden was not the final garden. There was Gethsemane, the garden where Mary came looking for her Lord's body. For a few moments that first Easter morning Mary thought she was talking to a gardener—not to Jesus. Actually, it was the new Gardener— Jesus, the second Adam. By His cross the curse was erased, and by His resurrection we begin again.

And that, of course, is the good news. It means that, in Christ, the curse vanishes. It means that, in Christ, sexuality can be redeemed to become, again, the means of the most intimate and fulfilling union between a couple. "The old has passed away; behold, the new has come."

PERSONAL
LOG:

Description and Log: Session 8

GOAL SETTING AND FINANCIAL PLANNING

SESSION
OVERVIEW: By reviewing role expectations and beginning a five-year financial plan, couples will identify some financial and career goals—and areas where differences exist.

SESSION
OUTCOME: Couples should be able to anticipate and negotiate some differences in financial and career goals.

Couples should have some knowledge of, and should value a process for, mutual goal setting.

THEOLOGICAL
REFLECTION: "Commit your work to the Lord, and your plans will be established" (Proverbs 16:3).

Few situations make us as vulnerable to others as a discussion of our most personal goals (our hopes, our dreams, our aspirations).

If people think our goals are foolish, we risk their mockery. If people think our goals are unworthy, we risk their contempt.

Besides, admitting our goals makes us vulnerable to failure. If we never confide our hopes in anyone, we may never have to acknowledge our disappointments. We simply pass through life repeating the slogan, "I didn't want that anyway . . . ."

And even if others both approve our goals and see us achieving them, our goals make us vulnerable because they represent—with terrifying clarity—what we genuinely *value*. Whatever we value (money, service, ourselves), our goals will immediately reveal our values.

Some people think a couple must hold the same goals, more or less, in areas of finance and planning. Perhaps the writer of Proverbs, though, reflects the more typical biblical emphasis which is on the *quality* of goals rather than their similarity. And he offers a simple guideline for measuring quality: any goal which can be committed to the Lord is worthy; any goal that can't is inappropriate.

Imagine how terribly vulnerable we'd all be if we knew every goal of every person in this group. Imagine how clearly everyone would know what you really value. Now imagine God is here.

PERSONAL
LOG:

DESCRIPTION AND LOG: SESSION 9

WHERE WE GO FROM HERE

SESSION
OVERVIEW: Couples will review their logs, select strengths and one area of weakness in their relationship, and outline a plan for action after the workshop.

SESSION
OUTCOME: Participants should be able to summarize what they have learned during this workshop.

Couples should commit themselves to a plan by which one area of weakness in their relationship can be strengthened before marriage, using skills learned during this workshop.

THEOLOGICAL
REFLECTION: "The grace of the Lord Jesus Christ and the love of God and the fellowship of the Holy Spirit be with you all" (2 Corinthians 13:14).

"The grace of the Lord Jesus Christ. . . ." It means "generosity" (Christ's being generous with us), or "favor" (He does us a remarkable favor). From the word *grace* we also get the word we translate "gifts," or *charismata* in Greek. A better translation of that word might be "graces"—what we show each other in workshops or in marriage when we are filled with Christ's *charis*.

". . . and the love of God. . . ." The Greek word which we translate "love" here is *agape* (a-gah'-pay). It means to love without worrying about whether we'll be loved in return. It means loving selflessly, becoming vulnerable. It means climbing up on a cross. It means being able to say, "You're forgiven."

". . . And the fellowship of the Holy Spirit be with you all." For "fellowship" the Greek word is *koinonia* (coin'-know-knee'-a). It means that sharing isn't really something we do with our words but with our burdens. It means that even the indecently ugly woman, even the vomit-drenched alcoholic, even the child abuser, and even the rapist—even these find room in the hearts of the Pentecost crowd. It means perfect union between imperfect people who have been born again by the Spirit.

You know these words as a benediction for your church. But today they are a benediction for your marriage.

If your marriage is marked by *charis* and *agape* and *koinonea*, you will experience precisely what you need for this time together.

PERSONAL
LOG:

Sample Evaluation Form

1. What was the most helpful part of the weekend for you?

2. What part of the experience could be improved? In what way?

3. What issues were not adequately dealt with?

4. How were the physical arrangements?

5. What feedback would you give us as to the leadership role? (positive and negative)

6. Any further comments or suggestions?

CHAPTER
6

Follow-up

CHAPTER 6

Follow-up

There is a great diversity of attitudes, values, and prior experience that individuals bring to their relationships, and those relationships are not fixed (in *any* sense of that word) in a single marriage preparation workshop. Some couples will need to work through special problems resulting from cultural and religious differences. Others will struggle with the kinds of identity changes that take place when two people marry at an early age and find themselves experiencing considerable role and career adjustment. Many young people look at marriage as a fluid relationship; they experience fear and anxiety as they struggle to build a satisfying and workable life style.

With the increasing rate of divorce and remarriage, extra effort is needed by those in the community of faith to help these marriageable persons understand and accept the failures of the past and to celebrate hope and forgiveness for the future.

Though this manual is intended as a resource for leading a group marriage preparation, it may be helpful for the leader to consider some of the following suggestions for follow-up, premarital counseling and education with individual couples.

1. An Outline for Premarital Counseling

The number and length of sessions will vary with the particular couple's level of preparation and the schedule of the counselor. The following outline is based on five one-and-one-half-hour sessions, beginning at least three months before the wedding ceremony. Specific information about additional resources may be found in the "Bibliography" and the section called "Additional Resources."

SESSION ONE:

1. Build the relationship by exploring the way the couple met, how they made their decision to marry, and the need-satisfying basis for the relationship.
2. Share data on the particulars of the wedding: wedding party, rehearsal, marriage license, physical checkups, etc.
3. Explore the meaning and function of the wedding ceremony, the role of the minister, the possibility of the couple's helping fashion the wedding liturgy.
4. Give or recommend a book about the marriage relationship to be read or discussed by the couple concurrent with the period of the premarital sessions.

Homework: Complete a premarital inventory, and spend time together sorting out the areas most important to be explored by you as a couple.

Note: Some counselors prefer to have the couple do the inventory prior to the first session so that compatibility issues may be explored at the beginning. The author's preference is to do some relationship building with the couple first. Some inventories are counterproductive if they are discussed at the outset, when there may be a high level of anxiety about the counseling relationship.

SESSION TWO:

1. Work with the couple on the basic formation of the wedding celebration.
2. Focus on the premarital inventory (similarities and differences), especially in areas that seem most significant to the couple.
3. Based on session observations, give each partner feedback

about his or her style of relating and communicating. Explore these patterns.

Homework: Give cassette tapes on sexual relating for private listening. Give or recommend a book on sexual relating and technique to be read and discussed by the couple. Some couples will feel free to discuss specific concerns with the minister, and others will not.

SESSION THREE:

1. Open the session with agenda material from the couple's reading; ask about concerns they're experiencing in their relationship. (Discussing the issue involving present relationships is often very productive.)
2. Spend considerable time finalizing plans for the wedding ceremony. Especially explore the spiritual and psychological significance of leaving one's father and mother and of cleaving to one another.

SESSION FOUR:

1. Review roles and communication patterns. Suggested resource: "MATE: An Inventory," focusing on role expectations (see No. 10 under "Bibliography").
2. Explore other issues important to the couple.
3. Schedule follow-up session.

SESSION FIVE: (Four to six weeks after the wedding ceremony)

Just as a new car needs a six-month maintenance check, so it's important that the counselor continue his or her pastoral care through a follow-up interview with the couple. Some couples prefer to have these interviews during regular intervals in the first few years of marriage. It is often after the initial four to six months of marriage that couples have generated some reality-based issues to be used for further relationship building.

2. Couple Communication and Enrichment

The "Bibliography" and the section called "Additional Resources" contain several suggestions for individual programs that couples may use at home to strengthen communication and enrich their relationships. A minister or a lay leader working in family life could develop a follow-up program for newly married couples. Such a program could provide opportunity for periodic marriage enrichment weekends or for some other format in which couples could find support for their early years of marriage. Group sessions could also be designed for feedback, with couples using these individual resources. The programmed guides vary from one to ten sessions in blocks of a half-hour to two hours (see No. 6 under "Bibliography").

3. Marriage Preparation and Family Life Education

a. The total church program should offer—as a regular part of the junior high, senior high, and young adult curricula— periodic courses which give young people an opportunity to think through the issues surrounding a biblical life style—a biblical view of sexuality, marriage, and the family.

b. A sound education program becomes the foundation for such growth experiences as the following:
    (1) Group marriage preparation workshops for couples.
    (2) Marriage enrichment workshops.
    (3) Expectant parents' groups.
    (4) Parents of young children groups.
    (5) Other parental groups.
    (6) Single parent groups.
    (7) Marriage enrichment for the middle and later years.
    (8) Family cluster education.

4. Association of Couples for Marriage Enrichment

"Graduates" of marriage preparation workshops should be encouraged to join organizations such as ACME, the Association of Couples for Marriage Enrichment, the stated purpose of which is to advance the cause of better marriages. Clergy and lay persons will also find that the ACME program offers an opportunity for developing leadership skills for marriage preparation and marriage enrichment training.

> ACME
> North American Office
> P.O. Box 10596
> Winston-Salem, NC 27108
> Telephone: (919) 724-1526

"Graduates" could also be encouraged through an area newsletter dedicated to enriching marriage and family life.

5. The Bibliography of Marriage Resources

The "Bibliography" is annotated and selectively chosen to provide a resource basis in this manual. But it is also intended to acquaint potential leaders with basic tools for marriage preparation, marriage enrichment, and marriage counseling.

This listing of resources does not imply unlimited endorsement by the author.

CHAPTER
7

Additional
Resources

PREMARITAL COMMUNICATION INVENTORY

This inventory offers you an opportunity to make an objective study of communication between you and your fiancé. It is designed to help couples learn more about themselves in preparation for marriage; it should help you become more objective about your readiness for marriage.

DIRECTIONS

1. The word *fiancé(e)* will be used to refer to the person to whom you are engaged or are considering as a possible marriage partner.

2. Please do not consult your fiancé while completing this inventory.

3. Your answers are confidential, and since your name is not required on this page, please be as frank as possible. Honest answers are very necessary if this form is to be of any value.

4. There is no time limit, but please answer each question as quickly as you can according to the way you feel *at the moment.*

5. Start with the following examples for practice. By putting a check ☑ in *one* of the three blanks on the right, you show how the question applies to you. Read the questions, and make your marks now. There are no right or wrong answers.

	YES usually	NO seldom	SOME-TIMES
Does your fiancé tell you his/her problems?	☐	☐	☐
Does your fiancé become angry when you do not agree with him/her?	☐	☐	☐

6. The YES column is to be used when the question can be answered as happening *most of the time* or *usually*. The NO column is to be used when the question can be answered as *seldom* or *never*.

   The SOMETIMES column should be marked when you definitely cannot answer YES or NO, but *use this column as little as possible.*

7. Read each question carefully, yet do not take too much time. If you cannot give the exact answer to a question, answer the best you can, but be sure to *answer each one.*

INVENTORY

	YES usually	NO seldom	SOME-TIMES
1. Do you and your fiancé discuss your differences?	☐	☐	☐
2. Do you have a tendency to keep your feelings to yourself?	☐	☐	☐
3. Do you and your fiancé quarrel very much?	☐	☐	☐

4. Does your fiancé tell you when he/she is angry with you? □ □ □

5. Does he/she stop seeing you without telling you why? □ □ □

6. Do you ever discuss your views about sex in marriage? □ □ □

7. Do the two of you settle your disagreements to your satisfaction? □ □ □

8. Do you find it difficult to talk with your fiancé? □ □ □

9. Do you find his/her tone of voice irritating? □ □ □

10. Do you discuss your attitudes toward premarital sexual relations? □ □ □

11. Does your fiancé fail to ask your opinion in making plans involving the two of you? □ □ □

12. Does he/she have a tendency to say things which would be better left unsaid? □ □ □

13. Do you find it necessary to keep after your fiancé for his/her faults? □ □ □

14. Do you communicate successfully with each others' families? □ □ □

15. Does it bother you *unduly* for your fiancé to express his/her own beliefs even if they differ from yours?   ☐   ☐   ☐

16. Do you understand his/her feelings and attitudes?   ☐   ☐   ☐

17. Does he/she seem to understand your feelings?   ☐   ☐   ☐

18. Does your fiancé nag you?   ☐   ☐   ☐

19. Do you think your fiancé is too critical of you?   ☐   ☐   ☐

20. Does your fiancé wait until you are through talking before saying what he/she has to say?   ☐   ☐   ☐

21. Do you refrain from saying something when you know it will only hurt your fiancé or make matters worse?   ☐   ☐   ☐

22. When a problem arises that needs to be solved, are you and your fiancé able to discuss it together (in a calm manner)?   ☐   ☐   ☐

23. Is your fiancé very jealous of you?   ☐   ☐   ☐

24. Are you very jealous of him/her?   ☐   ☐   ☐

25. Does he/she try to lift your spirits when you're depressed or discouraged?   ☐   ☐   ☐

26. Do you fail to express disagreement with your fiancé because you're afraid he/she will get angry? ☐ ☐ ☐

27. Are you and your fiancé able to disagree with one another without losing your tempers? ☐ ☐ ☐

28. Do you and your fiancé discuss how you will manage your money after you're married? ☐ ☐ ☐

29. Do you have disagreements over money now? ☐ ☐ ☐

30. Does he/she often say one thing but really mean another? ☐ ☐ ☐

31. Does your fiancé complain that you don't understand him/her? ☐ ☐ ☐

32. Do you help your fiancé to understand you by telling him/her how you think and feel about things? ☐ ☐ ☐

33. Do the two of you discuss what you expect of one another in terms of becoming a future mother and father? ☐ ☐ ☐

34. Do you neglect discussing what you expect of one another in terms of being a future husband and wife? ☐ ☐ ☐

35. Does your fiancé often sulk and pout? ☐ ☐ ☐

36. Do you feel that in most matters he/she knows what you are trying to say? ☐ ☐ ☐

37. Do you discuss your views on rearing children? ☐ ☐ ☐

38. Do the two of you fail to discuss your religious attitudes and beliefs? ☐ ☐ ☐

39. Do you discuss how far you want to go in petting? ☐ ☐ ☐

40. Is it easier to confide in a friend than in your fiancé? ☐ ☐ ☐

Please write the first thing that comes to your mind when you read the following words or phrases. Be honest with yourself in order to derive the maximum benefit from this evaluation.

1. What worries me most about marriage is _____

_____

_____

2. The thing I like the most about my fiancé is _____

_____

_____

3. The thing I like the least about my fiancé is _____

_____

_____

4. The biggest adjustment I may have to make in marriage is

_____

_____

_____

5. The hardest subject to discuss with my fiancé is _____

_____

_____

6. I get angry when _____

_____

_____

7. What puzzles me most about my fiancé is _____

_____

_____

8. As a communicator I would rate myself as:

Poor   Fair   Average   Good   Very Good

9. Looking back on my growing up, the type of communication I had with my parents was:

Poor   Fair   Average   Good   Very Good

10. In completing this questionnaire I was:

Very Frank   Frank   Not So Frank

General Information:

Your Age_____ Age of Fiancé _____ Sex: Male   Female

Your Education _____ Fiancé's Education _____

Your Occupation _____ Fiancé's Occupation _____

Your Religion _____ Fiancé's Religion _____

I grew up in: The country   Small town   Small city
                        Suburbs   Large city

Engaged?   Yes   No

How long have you been dating your fiancé?   _____

Were you previously married?   Yes   No

AGREE-DISAGREE STATEMENTS FOR GROUPS

INSTRUCTIONS: Read each statement once. Check whether you agree (A) or disagree (B) with each statement. Take about four minutes for deciding on the ten statements. Then in small groups try to agree or disagree unanimously with each statement as a *group*. Try especially to discover reasons for disagreement. If your group cannot reach agreement or disagreement, you may change the wording in any statement enough to promote unanimity.

KEY: "A" if you agree
"B" if you disagree

(   ) 1. Love is often a violent and uncontrollable emotion.

(   ) 2. Difference in social class and religion are of small importance as compared with love in selecting a marriage partner.

(   ) 3. As long as you really love a person, you will be able to solve the problems you have with that person.

(   ) 4. As long as one really loves another person, any flaws in his or her personality can be readily changed.

(   ) 5. Sometimes, ignoring the feelings of your partner is necessary for a smooth functioning marriage.

(   ) 6. It is often necessary to change the person in the direction you think is right.

(   ) 7. The experience one has had previous to marriage seldom effects how a person acts in the marital relationship.

(   ) 8. There is no such thing as a happily married couple.

(   ) 9. Sexual adjustment in marriage is always a difficult matter.

(   ) 10. If a couple get along reasonably well in marriage, they will never need to see a marriage counselor.

SAMPLE BUDGETS

YEAR-END REVIEW FOR CALENDAR YEAR 198 __

Income for the twelve months, including
investment income $_____

Spent on living, a total of $_____

Paid in federal and state income taxes
(and city wage taxes) $_____

Added to savings and investments,
and/or repaid on general debts $_____

      Total $_____

TOTAL OF 12 MONTHS' SPENDING
(Excludes Savings and Taxes)

	Total Actually Spent for Year	Compared with Spending Plan for Year
Food	$ _____	$ _____
Housing	_____	_____
Clothing	_____	_____
Medical Care	_____	_____
Transportation	_____	_____
Advancement	_____	_____
Gifts	_____	_____
Personal care	_____	_____
Entertainment	_____	_____

Allowances,
   miscellaneous   _____   _____

Life insurance   _____   _____

        Totals $ _____ $ _____

Resource materials:

HOW MUCH DEBT CAN YOU AFFORD?

MONTHLY INCOME

  Take-home Pay $ _____
  Other Income $ _____

                       $ _____   _____

  Total Income $ _____
MONTHLY EXPENSES (fixed)

  Mortgage or Rent $ _____
  Life Insurance   _____
  House Insurance   _____
  Auto Insurance   _____
  Local Taxes   _____
  Other $ _____
                      $ _____ $ _____

MONTHLY EXPENSES (variable)

  Utilities $ _____
  Medical (including health
     insurance)   _____
  Food   _____
  Clothing, Laundry,
     and Cleaning   _____
  Recreation   _____

Furnishings and Other
  Household Expenses   _____
Church Contributions   _____
Savings, Investments   _____
Other $ _____
            $ _____   _____

    TOTAL EXPENSES $ _____
    TOTAL MONTHLY INCOME $ _____
    TOTAL MONTHLY EXPENSES $ _____

Your Monthly Debt-Payment Limit $ _____

YOUR PRESENT DEBTS

PURPOSE OF LOAN   Balance due

Car $ _____
Home modernization   _____
Household Equipment
  and Appliances   _____
Charge Accounts   _____
Other $ _____
            $ _____   _____
    TOTAL $ _____

To check whether you are operating within a safe debt-payment limit, figure your present debt load in the bottom section of the form. If you want to use the twelve-month safety rule, the total amount left to pay should not exceed twelve times your monthly installments total.

Your credit is based upon (1) payment *performance* on past loans, (2) *intention* to repay (your stability and honesty), and (3) your *ability* to repay (your income level when borrowing).

Bibliography

Bibliography

1. Understanding Marriage

Beck, D. F., *Marriage and the Family Under Challenge: An Outline of Issues, Trends and Alternatives*, second edition. New York: Family Service Association of America, 1976.

A convenient overview of current trends in marriage and family life with an excellent annotated bibliography of important journal articles and some books.

Bernard, Jessie. *The Future of Marriage.* New York: World, 1972.

This book is useful in helping the pastor or the counselor view the cultural background of the couple in preparation for looking at the shape of the marriage in the future. It is especially helpful in presenting a brief history of marriage and in exploring sex roles.

Bower, Robert. *Solving Problems in Marriage.* Grand Rapids: Wm. B. Eerdmans, 1972.

This book is written for all Christian couples who want a stronger and better marriage—not just for those whose marriage is in jeopardy. The assumption behind this book is that if couples will read about the nature, stresses, conflicts, and basic dynamics of marriage, they can begin to gain greater insight into their own situation and thereby contribute to the solution of the problems confronting them. The author presents a happy balance between the psychological and the theological dimensions of marital stress.

167

Clinebell, Howard and Charlotte. *The Intimate Marriage.* New York: Harper & Row, 1970.

This resource opens up levels of marriage in which partners can work constructively together and suggests techniques that can be used. It deals with emotional, intellectual, sexual, spiritual, and creative aspects of relationships. A "Talk it over" section after each chapter is useful for discussion groups.

Demarest, Gary. *Christian Alternatives Within Marriage.* Waco, Tex.: Word, 1977.

A book designed for discussion and study groups of couples over an eight session period with accompanying study questions.

Fairchild, Roy. *Christians in Families.* Richmond, Va.: CLC Press, 1964.

One of the best books that seek to define the nature and mission of the Christian family. There are excellent chapters on "Looking at Marriage Through the Eyes of Faith" and "The Sexual Revolution: A New Challenge."

Godard, J. M. *The Blue Light, Christian Dimensions in Marriage.* Richmond, Va.: CLC Press, 1964.

This book is designed to help readers discover unique Christian dimensions in marriage. The book will help readers realize what God intends for them in marriage.

Granberg, Lars I. *For Adults Only.* Grand Rapids: Zondervan, 1971.

This book deals with the current stresses and strains being placed on married life in the twentieth century. It emphasizes that the teachings of the Bible concerning humankind, personal relations, and marriage and family life contain true and workable answers for persons today as well as in the earlier centuries.

Hanaghan, Jonathon. *The Courage to Be Married.* St. Meinrod, Ind.: Abbey, 1974.

This is a lively and stirring discussion of the dynamics of marriage from the viewpoint of an Irish psychoanalyst and poet. The book is most exciting in its fresh and passionate treatment of the spiritual adventure of marriage.

Langsdale, Richard. *Getting Ready for Living Together.* Philadelphia: Fortress, 1974.

This is a clever, down-to-earth, and helpful, brief book about building and enriching marriage, written by a Lutheran counselor and pastor.

La Rossa, Ralph. *Conflict and Power in Marriage: Expecting the First Child.* Beverly Hills, Calif.: Sage, 1977.

A useful in-depth study of the transition from the beginning to the end of pregnancy, with ample case history material.

Lederer, William J., and Don D. Jackson. *The Mirages of Marriage.* New York: W. W. Norton, 1968.

This is an excellent book that enables a person to understand marriage as an interlocking system, as well as providing some techniques for dealing with destructive elements in marriage. The authors believe that if a marriage is going to work, the husband and wife will need to be primarily responsible for their own behavior and growth in relationship to each other.

Lee, Robert, and Marjorie Casebier. *The Spouse Gap: Weathering the Marriage Crisis During Middlescence.* Nashville: Abingdon, 1971.

Here is a book that will help couples adjust to "the empty nest," enabling them to reassess their roles and find new directions for creative living.

Leslie, Gerald R. and Elizabeth M. *Marriage in a Changing World.* New York: John Wiley, 1977.

A functionally oriented very readable treatment of the current research in changing family lifestyles.

Mace, David. *Getting Ready for Marriage.* Nashville: Abingdon, 1972.

A book by an internationally known authority on marriage and family life that will help young people prepare for marriage. Dr. Mace tries to deal with young people in this book as though he were counseling them about "What You Bring to Each Other" and "What You Must Do To Succeed."

Mace, David and Vera. *We Can Have Better Marriages If We Really Want Them.* Nashville: Abingdon, 1974.

Here is a challenge to the current disillusionment about marriage and an outline of a way for couples to make their marriages healthier, stronger, more joyous, and better able to serve the needs of both the couple and society as a whole.

McCary, J. L. *Freedom and Growth in Marriage.* Santa Barbara: Hamilton Co., 1975.

A book highlighting the importance of individual growth and development as a significant component of the total marriage relationship.

McGinnis, C. *Your First Year of Marriage.* New York: Doubleday, 1967.

Helpful reading for couples as a part of a premarital counseling program.

Osborne, Cecil. *The Art of Understanding Your Mate* (with Leader's Guide). Grand Rapids: Zondervan, 1979.

A practical discussion of the adjustments of married life; useful in small groups.

Otto, Herbert A. *More Joy in Your Marriage.* New York: Hawthorn, 1969.

This is an action book! It is designed to help you have more joy together through doing—not through reading. At the end of each chapter are suggestions for couples, and in Appendix J are suggestions for couples' groups.

Perry, John and Erma. *Pairing and Parenthood: An Introduction to Marriage and the Family.* San Francisco: Canfield Press, 1977.

A basic text in the field—factual, straightforward, presenting many sides of controversial issues in terms which communicate well with today's youth.

Peterson, James H. *Married Love in the Middle Years.* New York: Association Press, 1968.

This is a good study book for husbands and wives whose children have matured and are about to leave home. This book deals with ways of how husband and wife can discover the richer joys of maturity.

Powell, John. *The Secret of Staying In Love.* Niles, Ill.: Argus Communications, 1974.

This book deals with practical ways of developing a better communication system between persons who are in love. After emphasizing the need for the honest sharing of feelings and emotions, some practical exercises are included in the last chapter.

Rogers, Carl R. *Becoming Partners: Marriage and Its Alternatives.* New York: Dell, 1972.

This book is a frank look into the lives of people in both traditional and nontraditional relationships. The reader has an opportunity to make his or her own value judgments as well as to profit from Rogers' keen insights into successful relationships.

Simons, Joseph, and Reidy, Jeanne. *The Risk of Loving.* New York: Seabury, 1973.

This book is full of interesting and very real pictures of the process of building interpersonal relationships, whether they are between married people or single individuals. It has excellent chapters on loneliness, possessiveness, and sensitivity.

Tournier, Paul. *To Understand Each Other.* Richmond, Va.: John Knox, 1973.

Marriage insights for couples who "live side by side, without hurting one another, but poles apart because of no real understanding of one another."

2. Sex and Marriage

Eichenlaub, John E. *The Marriage Act.* New York: Dell, 1961.

This book has remained as an excellent, inexpensive guide to sexual technique in the context of a growing relationship. The focus is upon the couple in their growing sexual fulfillment.

Hollis, Harry, Jr. *Thank God For Sex.* Nashville: Broadman, 1975.

This book affirms sex as God's gift. It interprets sexuality in terms of the biblical concepts of creation, judgment, and redemption. It also emphasizes the need for celebration, self-discipline, and love. This book examines the current exploitation of human sexuality and then reflects on the beauty of sex as a gift of God.

Hulst, Hugo L. *A Search for Meaning, Love, Sex and Marriage.* Winona, Minn.: St. Mary's College Press, 1970.

This resource is best used in group discussions. It is accompanied by a helpful teaching guide.

Mace, David. *The Christian Response to the Sexual Revolution.* Nashville: Abingdon, 1970.

An excellent book that begins with biblical references to sex and shows how some basic misconceptions about sex have become accepted Christian principles. He encourages Christians to think about their sexual attitudes and urges the church to reevaluate its teachings so that it may respond in an authentic manner to the challenge of the sexual revolution.

———. *Sexual Difficulties in Marriage.* Philadelphia: Fortress, 1971.

An excellent booklet that takes the learnings from the Taylor-Johnson research projects and puts them into understandable language.

Masters, William A., and Johnson, Virginia E. *The Pleasure Bond.* Boston: Little, Brown, 1974.

A good book on the ways in which the loving and caring sexual relationship of a couple can be strengthened and intensified as time goes by. Available in paperback.

Morrison, Eleanor A., and Price, Mila U. *Values in Sexuality.* New York: Hart, 1974.

This is a helpful resource to the workshop leader or educator in designing value clarification exercises for couples.

Piper, Otto. *The Biblical View of Sex and Marriage.* New York: Scribner, 1960.
This book gives a comprehensive, biblical study of both sex and marriage. If someone desires to do a serious, biblical study in the area of sex and marriage, this book becomes a must. This book is a follow-up to an earlier book by Dr. Piper on *The Christian Interpretation of Sex.*

Small, Dwight H. *Christian: Celebrate Your Sexuality.* Old Tappan, N.J.: Revell, 1974.
This book is a fresh, positive approach to understanding and fulfilling sexuality.

Smedes, Lewis B. *Sex for Christians: The Limits and Liberties of Sexual Living.* Grand Rapids: Wm. B. Eerdmans, 1976.
This book provides biblical perspective in a Reformed and contemporary style. It is easily understood by most couples and is widely recognized as a most helpful resource. It contains sections on "Sex and Christian People," "Sex and Single People," "Sex and Married People." Smedes is Professor of Theology and Philosophy of Religion at Fuller Theological Seminary.

Stroup, Herbert, Jr., and Wood, Norma S. *Sexuality and the Counseling Pastor.* Philadelphia: Fortress, 1974.
A very helpful treatment of the Christian tradition and human sexuality, with a section on the pastor's own sexuality. The authors raise hard questions with controversial responses in the section on human sexuality outside the coupled world.

Tapes:

Human Development Institute
20 Executive Park West, N.E.
Atlanta, GA 39329

Overcoming Sexual Inadequacy, Stephen Neiger.

These twelve cassettes are useful in premarital situations where there are certain fears and problems centered around sexuality. The tapes are most helpful in marriage counseling. This is an extremely comprehensive series on almost every area of sexuality.

Sex Techniques and Sex Problems. Ed Wheat, M.D.

A two-cassette three-hour, excellent discussion of the physiology of sex, sex technique, sexual problems, and the emotional aspects of lovemaking.

For information on birth control it is recommended that the couple refer to their doctor's most up-to-date resources. One resource for physicians: Budlong Press, 5428 N. Virginia Avenue, Chicago, IL 60625

3. Financial Help

Several useful booklets are available from the following:

Women's Division
Institute of Life Insurance
227 Park Avenue
New York, NY 10017

The booklets are "A Discussion of Family Money," "Why So Broke," "Young Couples Make Money Work," and "You and Your Family's Life Insurance."

Margolius, Sidney. "Family Money Problems." Public Affairs Pamphlet No. 412, 381 Park Avenue South, New York, NY 10016.

Reeves, J.; Kelson, V.; and Daly, Ronald. "Personal Money Management." University Associates, 7596 Eads Avenue, La Jolla, CA 92037.

This is a project book and plan book containing self-assessment questionnaires, financial forms, and twenty-four practical treatments of various aspects of personal finances.

4. Career Resources

Career Planning Consultants, Inc.
2120 Toy Road
Charlottesville, VA 22901

List of resources available on request.

Lifework Planning. Arthur and Marie Kirn. "Finding Out About Your Work and Your Life" and "Putting It All Together." University Associates, 7956 Eads Avenue, La Jolla, CA 92037.

Effective Personal and Career Decision Making. Bartsh, Yost and Girrell, Career Planning Center, Penn State University, State College, PA 16801.

Bolles, Dick. *Quick Job-Hunting Map* and *What Color Is Your Parachute?* Life/Work Planning Center, Barat College, Lake Forest, IL 60045.

Both are excellent career resources based on the latest information and career research.

5. Marriage Preparation Resources

Phillips, Clinton E., and Pixley, Erma. *A Guide For Premarriage Counseling,* Los Angeles: American Institute of Family Relations, 1963.

This small pamphlet provides a basic framework for four premarital counseling sessions. It also contains some helpful suggestions along with a bibliography that would help a counselor meet specific needs of individual couples.

Engaged Encounter Manual. National Marriage Encounter, 955 Lake Drive, St. Paul, MN 55120.

This weekend-for-marriage-preparation grows out of the popular Catholic Marriage Encounter Movement. The focus is upon learning from the experience of married couples and individual couple dialogue.

Gangsei, L. B. *Manual for Group Pre-Marital Counseling,* New York: Association Press, 1971.

An alternative group model for working with couples in a religious setting.

Marriage Counseling Kit. James R. Hine. Interstate Printers
    and Publishers, Inc., Danville, IL 61832.

A card-sorting "game" designed to create a situation in which the
young couple freely reveal some important factors about themselves
in terms of their coming marriage. It enables couples to discuss
differences of opinion and enables the counselor to evaluate both
the strong and weak points in their relationship.

Rolfe, David J. *Marriage Preparation Manual.* New York:
    Paulist Press, 1975.

This is a structured minilecture-discussion model with excellent
detailed instructions for a one-day or two-afternoon plan. Professionals and paraprofessionals are used in a carefully coordinated
way.

Mosaic Series. 1972. Novalis, 1 Stewart Street, Ottawa,
    Canada, K1N 8V7.

This series is used extensively as homework in the "Rolfe program."
Seven topic areas in booklet form are designed to help couples at
home explore such areas as roles, building closeness, sexuality, par-
enting, handling differences.

*The Christian Faces Emotions, Marriage, and Family Re-
    lationships.* H. Norman Wright. Christian Marriage En-
    richment, 5777 East Evans Avenue, Suite 1, Denver,
    CO 80222.

This curriculum resource includes a section outlining a six session
approach to group premarital counseling and marriage preparation
to accompany the taped series, *Upon This Foundation.* The design
is one of sharing information with couple response and group discussion.

To Love and to Cherish. Nashville: Methodist Publishing
    House, 1970.

This is a manual that has been prepared to help Methodist pastors
conduct their premarital conferences. The book contains a helpful
theology of marriage along with some practical concepts that ought
to be part of a premarital conference. There is also available a reading book for engaged couples to use by the same title.

Two As One, A Christian Marriage Preparation Program,
Manual and Workbook. Margin G. Olsen and George E.
Von Kaenel. New York: Paulist Press, 1976.

These materials are used in the Christian Marriage Preparation Program, a series of three informal sessions within a week's time to help engaged couples prepare themselves for marriage. A team of two married couples and a clergyman act as facilitators. Special training for facilitators is an important part of the effectiveness of this experientially based program.

Upon This Foundation, Volume I, "Marriage Preparation and
Premarital Counseling." H. Norman Wright. Christian
Marriage Enrichment, 5777 East Evans Avenue, Suite
1, Denver, CO 80222.

A cassette series that will help the busy pastor better prepare himself for premarital counseling. It gives directions for using the "Taylor-Johnson Temperament Analysis Test" as well as for using other tools for counseling. These cassettes should be used to upgrade the pastor skills rather than in the premarital counseling setting itself.

The May 1976 issue of *The Christian Ministry* is devoted
entirely to marriage preparation. There are many ideas
for clergy as well as an article by Stanley Rock and T. N.
Tormey on a couple-centered approach to premarriage
education.

6. Marriage Enrichment Resources

Cassettes and Programmed Guides:

Alive and Aware: Improving Communication in Relationships.
Interpersonal Communication Programs, Inc., 300 Clifton Avenue, Minneapolis, MN 55403, 1975. Text and
Couple's Workbook available.

This is a carefully designed fourteen-hour skill-building program tested over many years through the University of Minnesota Couple Communication project. Instructors can be secured through ICP to offer the program in your church or community.

Building a Christian Marriage. Bruce and Hazel Larson. Creative Resources, Box 1790, Waco, TX 76703. One cassette and response guide.

A uniquely designed one-hour workshop on developing a creative marital relationship. This course contains probing questions and activities you and your spouse can actually have fun doing together.

Communication: Key To Your Marriage. Norm Wright with Fritz Ridenour. Regal Press, Glendale, CA 91209, 1974.

Learning packet includes learning guide, book, and cassette resource for ten sessions. This is a book, along with a cassette resource guide, designed not only to teach communication skills but to encourage couples to use these skills. Some basic, biblical principles related to good communication patterns are outlined.

Growth Counseling-Enriching Marriage and Family. Howard and Charlotte Clinebell. Abingdon Press, Nashville, TN 37202. Four cassettes and user's guide.

This is a do-it-yourself cassette course for learning human development approaches to helping others and yourself. The tapes are intended to move the pastor from a diagnostic-sickness approach to a human development and fulfillment approach in counseling. Dr. Clinebell believes that the growth model for counseling enables the church-related counselor to use more of his natural assets in the growth of "normal" people throughout the life cycle. A user's guide accompanies these cassettes.

Guide to Family Ministries. Philadelphia: Geneva Press, 1975.

Along with other resources for Family Life Ministry, this pamphlet contains a Suggested Marriage Enrichment Program written by Del and Trudy Vander Haar. This section provides background information on why the church needs to be involved in marriage enrichment as well as a model that can be developed by skilled facilitators for use in such a program.

Improving Communication in Marriage. 5th ed., 1971. Human Development Institute, 20 Executive Park West, N.E., Atlanta, GA 30329.

This is a programmed instruction course designed to be taken by a husband and wife together. There are eight one-half to one-hour sessions, planned generally for weekend use. The course is designed to be taken by ordinary couples in a face-to-face style with the goal of helping a couple build more effective communication skills.

Intimacy. Human Development Institute, 20 Executive Park West, N.E., Atlanta, GA 30329.

A program of encountering experiences for husband and wife to enjoy together. Each session lasts two hours, covering such areas as opening up, listening, paining, touching, risking, and growing. Cassette and booklets are used together. Excellent homework for couples who are in marriage counseling.

Living Married. Cooperative Extension Services, Curtice Hall, Iowa State University, Ames, IA 50010, 1976.

A very useful discussion guide produced for an education television series of the same name. Free or at nominal cost.

Otto, Herbert A., ed. *Marriage and Family Enrichment.* Nashville: Abingdon, 1976.

This book is a gold mine of excellent material for all kinds of marriage and family programming in church and community, including marriage enrichment programs developed by RCA persons—Del and Trudy Vander Haar, Bud and Bea Van Eck.

7. Resource Newsletters
ACME Newsletter

Christian Marriage Enrichment–Marriage and Family Resource Newsletter. Christian Marriage Enrichment, 5777 East Evans Avenue, Denver, CO 80222.

A newsletter that identifies current resources for marriage and family life. Published ten times a year.

8. Marriage Counseling

Ard, Ben and Constance, eds. *Handbook of Marriage Counseling.* Palo Alto: Science and Behavior Books, 1971.

This comprehensive volume combines the wisdom of thirty-two of the most distinguished counselors and scholars in the field of marriage and family relations. It is an excellent resource book for a pastor who wants to update his professional counseling skills.

Barry, W. A., et al. *Communication, Conflict and Marriage.* Palo Alto: Science and Behavior Books, 1971.

Helpful to the counselor in providing a theoretical framework for identifying persistent conflict patterns in couple relationships.

Bird, J. W. *Marriage is for Grownups.* New York: Doubleday, 1969.

This book takes a problem-solving approach to common marriage conflicts and examines traditional sex roles and stereotypes.

Clinebell, Howard. *Basic Types of Pastoral Counseling.* Nashville: Abingdon, 1966.

This is a basic textbook for a pastor to use for improving his counseling skills. The book gives some insights on the uniqueness of pastoral counseling and suggests a style of counseling a pastor should use today. Two chapters relate in particular to marriage and family counseling.

Herigan, J. and Herigan, J. *Loving Free.* New York: Grosset and Dunlop, 1974.

This book is written by a couple who have rediscovered excitement and meaning in a marriage that had reached a dull plateau; useful for couple reading.

Hine, James R. *Marriage Counseling: A Guide For Ministers.* Danville, Ill.: Interstate Printers and Publishers.

This brief, concise discussion of the minister as marriage counselor covers such matters as what to do in the first interview, planning a program of counseling with an individual couple, helping a couple communicate, sex education for marriage, the importance of religious beliefs, etc. It also includes a bibliography of sixty-five books the author recommends to help in counseling.

_____. *Your Marriage: Analysis and Renewal.* Danville, Ill.: Interstate Printers and Publishers.

A guide to be used by marriage counselors, clergy, and couples desiring to make an inventory of their marriage for the purpose of evaluation and improvement.

Johnson, Dean. *Marriage Counseling: Theory and Practice.* Englewood Cliffs, N.J.: Prentice-Hall, 1961.

Though out of print, this is a basic book in the field and takes the reader step by step through the counseling process. There is generous case material with an excellent chapter on the beginning interview.

Knox, David. *Marriage Happiness, A Behavioral Approach to Counseling.* Champaign, Ill.: Research Press, 1972.

This book is particularly helpful in the counseling process when attention is being given to specific ways of bringing about behavioral change that may contribute to greater marital happiness. There is a useful precounseling questionnaire included in the appendixes.

Lasswell, M. and N. Lobsenz. *No Fault Marriage.* New York: Ballantine, 1976.

A very practical and readable discussion of making a marriage work in contemporary life.

Morris, J. Kenneth. *Marriage Counseling: A Manual for Ministers.* Englewood Cliffs, N.J.: Prentice-Hall, 1965.

This is a book by an experienced marriage counselor who writes with special sensitivity on the task of the minister-counselor. The book mainly looks at the counseling process through case histories from the author's practice. Morris has also written a helpful book in premarital counseling: *Premarital Counseling: A Manual for Ministers* (1960).

Satir, Virginia. *Conjoint Family Therapy.* Palo Alto: Science and Behavior Books, 1967.

This book still remains an excellent fundamental classic in understanding the importance of the whole family system in family counseling.

Stewart, C. W. *The Minister As Marriage Counselor,* rev. ed. New York: Abingdon, 1970.

This book will help a pastor gain new skills in the counseling process. The author deals with the social system of marriage and recognizes that marriage is a cluster of interpersonal relationships that need to be recognized by a counselor. He concludes the book with "A Theology of Marriage."

Wilke, Richard B. *The Pastor and Marriage Group Counseling.* Nashville: Abingdon, 1974.

This book is a fine attempt at encouraging the minister to consider a group marriage counseling approach, using the healing resources of the church's ministry in a small group context. The model is rooted in the author's experience in healing and renewal through Christian community.

Wright, H. Norman. *Upon This Foundation,* Vol. II, "Marriage and Family Counseling," Christian Marriage Enrichment, 5777 E. Evans Avenue, Suite 1, Denver, CO 80222.

Here's a series of six cassettes along with a resource guide for the counseling pastor. Several tapes deal with marriage counseling and the conducting of marriage seminars. Other tapes relate to "crisis counseling."

9. Films

Focus on Marriage. Study Guide on these films available from Concordia Publishing House, 3558 S. Jefferson Ave., St. Louis, MO 63118.

Handling Marital Conflicts. McGraw-Hill.

Though a bit old, this film is still a very fine tool for demonstrating positive and negative ways of resolving conflict through a look into the lives of two couples. B&W and Color. 14 min. Order from Michigan State University, Instructional Media Center, E. Lansing, MI 48824 or your local university.

Teleketic Marriage Series. Available individually from Travarca, Box 247, Grandville, MI 49418.

We Do! We Do!

On Taking the Step: Confronted by dire warning from friends and computers, a young couple about to be married reconsiders what it means to say, "I do." Color, 12 minutes.

You Haven't Changed a Bit

Adjusting to Marriage: After a quarrel a young married couple take separate vacations at home with their parents, only to discover that, although shaped by the past, their real identity lies in their future together. Color, 14 minutes.

The Weekend

The Middle Years: A rained-out weekend vacation becomes a time of rediscovery for a middle-aged couple whose lack of communication has driven them apart. Color, 16 minutes.

Encounter

Six one-minute spots that explore communication and interpersonal relationships as a basis of communication with man and God. Scripture text at the end of each scene relates it to our faith. Discussion guide helps groups to raise the right questions. Color.

Three Styles of Marital Conflict. Research Press, 2612 N. Mattis Avenue, Champaign, IL 61820.

An excellent film demonstrating through three different couples' interactions the most common patterns of marital conflict, with an emphasis on identifying the underlying "system" that reinforces destructive patterns in marriage. With leader's guide. Color, 14 minutes.

10. Psychological Tools and Marriage Inventories

Family Life Publications, Inc., Box 429, Saluda, NC 28773.

Here is a series of various tests that can be used by a pastor with discretion:

  a. Courtship Analysis
  b. Dating Problem Check List
  c. Love Attitudes Inventory

    d. Marriage Inventory
    e. Marriage Prediction Schedule
    f. Marriage Role Expectation Inventory
    g. Marriage Expectation Inventory

Research Press, 2612 N. Mattis Ave., Champaign, IL 61820.

Two excellent inventories that can be used in individual sessions and group settings, strongly behavioral in orientation:

    a. Premarital Counseling Inventory
    b. Marital Precounseling Inventory

Other Psychological Tests and Inventories

MATE. A Firo scale developed by William C. Schutz.

This instrument is designed to discover the ways in which partners satisfy each other and in what ways there are difficulties. It can be used both in premarital and marital counseling.

RELATIONSHIP INTIMACY BAROMETER (RIB), P. J. Mac Donald, MSW, et al., 1979.

A new instrument, quickly administered, providing an accurate indication of significant trends in a relationship, whether engaged, married or unformalized. Trends or positions in a relationship are measured by ten dimensions: love, satisfaction, feelings, similarities, competence, religion, communication, roles, sex and intimacy. This instrument promises to be an extremely useful "barometer" of where participants in a relationship position themselves in relation to one another.

    Scoring is done by computer through GMI, Ltd., 2745 Douglas Avenue, Des Moines, IA 50310. Accompanying workbook for programmed experience and teaching.

Taylor-Johnson Temperament Analysis Profile. Psychological Publications, Inc., 5300 Hollywood Blvd., Los Angeles, CA 90017.

References are necessary in order to qualify to purchase. Request the same from the Office of Family Life. This test ranks as one of the most respected tools among professional counselors. It measures nine personality traits. It can be given crisscross as well.